ON THE BOARDS
WITH BLOWERS

ON THE
BOARDS
WITH
BLOWERS

Peter Baxter

Matador
9 Priory Business Park,
Wistow Road, Kibworth Beauchamp,
Leicestershire. LE8 0RX
Tel: 0116 279 2299
Email: books@troubador.co.uk
Web: www.troubador.co.uk/matador
Twitter: @matadorbooks

ISBN 978 1838590 956

British Library Cataloguing in Publication Data.
A catalogue record for this book is available from the British Library.

Printed and bound in the UK by T J International, Padstow, Cornwall
Typeset in 11pt Minion Pro by Troubador Publishing Ltd, Leicester, UK

Matador is an imprint of Troubador Publishing Ltd

MIX
Paper from
responsible sources
FSC
www.fsc.org
FSC® C013056

For the loyal *Test Match Special* listeners
past, present and future.

Contents

Foreword

By Henry Blofeld

BLOFELD AND BAXTER MAY not have quite the same ring to it as Morecambe and Wise or Marks and Spencer, but for two hundred and more shows over about five years, we were a going concern and what fun it was. Our double acts were, if anything, a harder task for Backers, for he had produced me in the Test Match Special box for thirty-odd years, but now found that I was the senior partner, for I had done a bit of board-treading before we joined forces. To start with, at any rate, I was on the more familiar ground and he did heroically well to sit on his own producerly inclinations.

As usual I was all over the place, but Backers nobly bit his tongue and from time to time we certainly shook the occasional rafter while we were together. Sometimes we played to quite full houses, but there were others when a myriad of empty seats glared back at us. The reason I like to have stage lights turned up as far as possible so that I cannot see the audience, is that it is much easier to play to empty seats if you are unable to see that they are empty.

Neil O'Brien, my agent, saw that our act might lead to something and suddenly we found ourselves tiptoeing across, I think, rather than treading the boards. We had a splendid time, tinged in equal measure with laughter, apprehension, irritation – at the stupidity of people who refused to fill those empty seats and at theatres who invariably told us we had sold more seats than we had – and once or twice with blind panic, but never tears.

We did three years at the Edinburgh Festival. In the first, in the Pleasance Courtyard, we followed a show by Nick Helm, who really let his hair down. Backstage we spent our time climbing over the huge inflatable penises which played an important part in his show. I never thought I would be tripped up by a penis, but there we are. Our numbers built up reasonably well, but I can remember watching through a crack in the curtains and counting our audience as each one of them arrived. When we first arrived at three figures, my goodness me, it was a heady moment.

Valeria, my wife, came to all our shows and looked after the merchandise we sold in the foyers of the theatres. We drove thousands of miles, staying with friends and at up-ish-market B&Bs as well as an assortment of modest hotels in which it was usually wiser not to look under the bed, rather than discover what was hidden there. Finding our lodgings was always a bit of an adventure and Backers, the producer to the fore, always got there first and talked Valeria and me in over the last few miles.

When we moved eventually into the embrace of Emma Brünjes Productions, we even had a couple of shows in the

West End, at the Lyric in Shaftesbury Avenue and then at the Duchess in Covent Garden. Those gave us extremely jolly and packed audiences, who laughed in most of the right places. Behind the scenes the admirable Duchess is a rabbit warren and getting from my dressing room to the stage in time needed more than just a touch of luck. Sherpa Tenzing would have been an invaluable companion.

I think I must have driven Backers mad at least three times every show, but stoically he gritted his teeth and never flinched. Our relative success was more than anything the result of the popularity of Test Match Special and the faithfulness of its audience.

In this book Backers has got it right. We started on a wing and a prayer after one of my greatest friends, Michael Proudlock, who so sadly and suddenly put his cue in the rack late in 2018, said at lunch, when Backers and I were pulling each other's legs, that we ought to go public. As this conversation took place in The Surprise, Oscar Wilde's pub in Chelsea, it seemed rather a good omen.

In these pages, Backers tells some excellent stories, even though I have heard them before, which is not, I suppose, altogether surprising. I just hope you haven't. This is a book which brings it all most happily back to me and I think will give even the most stony-hearted a thoroughly good chuckle. Well done, Backers, on the stage and now off it.

Beginnings

On a cold early-March Sunday afternoon in 2013, the streets of Leamington Spa did not seem particularly welcoming. And I'd arrived there much too early, having overestimated the time needed to drive the short distance up the M40. Still, it gave me the opportunity for a cup of tea before I was due at the Assembly.

I found a tea shop – after all, at half past four it was very much teatime. So they were just closing up, of course.

The Assembly itself, a Victorian building, was locked up front and back and no posters advertised what the evening entertainment – if any – might be. I waited on the broad, windswept pavement outside.

At last a man did turn up and start to unlock the booking office, which appeared to double as a record shop. He looked surprised that anyone would be trying to get in. "It's only two old cricket blokes tonight," he said.

"Yes," I said, through chattering teeth. "I'm one of them."

This, in fact, was to be the twenty-eighth performance by the 'two old cricket blokes' – Blofeld and Baxter – in the course of our second season of shows.

It was not something I had really expected to find myself doing, well into my retirement after forty-two years at the BBC, thirty-four of them as producer of *Test Match Special*.

On a warm summer day, twenty-one months earlier, I had gone up to London to have lunch and a catch-up with all the gossip with Henry Blofeld in a Chelsea pub. Inevitably a lot of the old *TMS* stories started to tumble out over a glass or two of wine. Tales were told of the thirst of John Arlott and his inability to understand the request, "Just a small one please, John"; the pranks and dreadful puns of Brian Johnston (I think summer pudding was on the menu, prompting Johnners' old favourite, "Summer pudding, some are not!"); and the disorganisation and eternal lateness of Christopher Martin-Jenkins. Bizarre events on tours round the cricketing world probably also got a mention.

As the wine slipped down and the "Do you remember…?"s grew more outrageous, we were quietly joined by the pub's proprietor, Michael Proudlock, an old friend of Blowers'. In a lull, he spoke. "You two ought to be doing this on stage," he suggested.

I thought little of this remark. Blowers, though, had been doing a one-man show round the theatres of Britain for some years and so had a better idea of what might work. Very early in the New Year of 2012, he summoned me to meet his then agent, Neil O'Brien, over lunch to discuss the possibility of our doing a two-man show under the title *Memories of Test Match Special.* Neil seemed enthusiastic. After seeing him into a taxi, Henry and I repaired to the Chelsea Arts Club round the corner, to continue the discussion of the practicalities.

The atmosphere to create, we felt, was pretty much the one in which we now found ourselves: two old buffers in armchairs in a club. A passing friend offered the suggestion of a whisky decanter on the table between us. Blowers was initially horrified. "Oh, no," he said, "we would never drink on stage!" But I could see that the look was the thing, and so our first prop was devised. Over the next five-and-a-half years the decanter contained apple juice, cold tea, a vinegar-and-water solution and, by the end, when we had started actually drinking its contents, back to apple juice.

Of course the next thing was to draft some ideas of what we might actually talk about. A theme, we felt, was called for. We had the idea to add stories to the tale of the history of *Test Match Special's* development. How the first commentator, back in 1927, the Reverend Frank Gillingham, had played for Essex because, it had been suggested, he was born in Tokyo and Essex was the nearest first-class county. He was later to blot his copybook in a rain break at the Oval, describing the scene by reading out the advertising hoardings round the ground.

The father of the art of radio commentary, Howard Marshall, would have to get a mention, including the story of a time when the BBC was not allowed to broadcast from inside Lord's. Marshall had to rush at appointed times to a nearby flat, where a makeshift studio had been set up, in order to deliver his reports. On one occasion, just as he was about to start, a piano lesson began, all too audibly, in the flat next door. The engineer was quickly dispatched to beg for quiet. All would then have been well, but for the mother of the would-be virtuoso appearing in the middle of Marshall's account of the progress of the Test Match, demanding to know for how long the expensive lesson would be suspended.

On another occasion, so impressed was Marshall by the bowling of the great Australian Bill O'Reilly, that he recited, "As for the O'Reilly you speak of so highly, gor blimey, O'Reilly, you are bowling well!" This, in those more strait-laced times, produced a storm of letters protesting at his blasphemous language.

We felt that the 'synthetic' Test Match commentaries run by the Australian Broadcasting Commission during the Ashes series in England in 1934 and 1938 deserved to be included in the story. Commentators sitting in a studio in Sydney would mount an imagined real-time commentary as if they were at the ground, informed only by regular cables from their man at the match. This was how the great Australian commentator Alan McGilvray had started.

We would then have to introduce the names of E. W. Swanton and Rex Alston as we approached the birth of *TMS* itself in 1957 and the advent of Arlott and – a bit later – Johnston.

Neil O'Brien had quickly booked half a dozen dates following our January meeting, and he had also commissioned a caricature of the two of us from John

Ireland, who had done us both before in *TMS* groups. That was excellent and a splendid publicity tool, but it meant that now we really needed to get our act together – quite literally.

At this time my village in north Buckinghamshire was in the throes of fighting an attempt by some opportunistic developers to build a wind farm in a wholly inappropriate place very close to habitation. It was suggested to me by the campaign organisers that Henry and I might give our show a 'charity premier' in aid of the fighting fund. As we needed a dry run, it was an idea that suited us very well and the date was fixed for our first appearance. On Saturday 5th May 2012, Blofeld and Baxter would take to the stage for the first time at Liscombe Park with the show *Memories of Test Match Special*.

Over lunch in the village pub a few weeks before, we drew up some sort of running order for the stories, with the general theme of telling the story of the programme's development. In retrospect, that was probably too cerebral an idea to make for the best entertainment, but it was a starting point.

On the subject of starting points, I suggested a story that I had for some time been telling in after-dinner speeches and which, surprisingly, Blowers had not heard before. An old Welsh friend of ours, the commentator Alun Williams (his first name was pronounced 'Al-in'; as he would always tell you, "To rhyme with sin and gin", and, as he had A Levels in both subjects, he knew what he was talking about), despite making his name principally for covering rugby and the great state events, did his first-ever broadcast on cricket. It was a county game in Cardiff, but the Welsh Home Service (as it would have been then) did not have a broadcasting point at Cardiff Arms Park, where the game was being played. So at the close of play Alun had to rush for a bus to take him up the road to the BBC studios at Llandaff. He sat on the top deck, furiously writing his report and just getting it finished as the bus arrived at Llandaff. The first person he ran into there was the announcer who had the job of introducing him on the air. This man could see that Alun was nervous about his debut broadcast, so he offered some advice.

"The trick," he said, "is to memorise the first line of your report. If you get that off pat, everything will flow on perfectly."

"Oh, thanks," said Alun, and for the next few minutes he paced the corridor outside the studio, repeating over and over again, "I've just come back from Cardiff Arms Park, where Glamorgan are playing Hampshire."

At last the announcer said, "Time to go in."

They sat down in the studio opposite each other. The red light came on and the announcer said, "Now here's Alun Williams, who's just come back from Cardiff Arms Park, where Glamorgan are playing Hampshire."

And, rather lamely, Alun said, "I've just come back from Cardiff Arms Park, where Glamorgan are playing Hampshire..."

That went down well and it is always nerve-settling to get an early laugh. But the show at Liscombe was to be the only time we used those stories of the history of our business. The day after that debut performance, a friend who had been there rang me, saying that he had enjoyed it very much, but added, "Leave out the historical stuff."

Nonetheless, that chilly May evening in the packed-out deconsecrated old chapel at Liscombe was a great success and taught us what we could do, particularly bouncing random remarks and memories off each other. We had, in fact, barely stuck to our agreed running order, probably because, in the heat of battle, neither of us could remember it. (The organisers would have regarded it as successful, too, in that, three years later, the plans for the wind farm were scrapped.)

Some of our stories were of course already tried and tested in our individual talks and after-dinner speeches. I had one favourite, in which I sometimes used to modify the language for respectable mixed audiences. As I launched into it on this particular evening, I hadn't really decided whether to use the sanitised version. When the moment came, though, I just thought, *What the hell*, and went for it.

In 1993, England played a series of three Test Matches in India, followed by a series of One Day Internationals. One of these one-day games was in Bangalore, in the south of the country, to be followed, a couple of days later, by another in Jamshedpur in the north-east. It was a travel day we had seen on the itinerary in advance, with some dismay, because such days are never straightforward in India.

The day started with our being told that the flight that constituted the first leg of the journey was delayed for several hours, a not uncommon event in India. So we did not set off until mid afternoon. That first leg was a two-hour flight due north up the east coast to Calcutta, for which we were flown by a maniac. This became clear when, halfway up the coast, he came on the aircraft's public address system. "If you look out on the right-hand side," he said excitedly, "you will see the shadow of my beautiful aeroplane on the sea!"

His tone raised an element of concern about the forthcoming landing, with some justification as it turned out, because he banged the plane down into the tarmac at Dum Dum Airport, Calcutta and, having inadvertently left his microphone switched on, treated us all to a scream which provoked discussion amongst his passengers. Was it a howl of terror, or a yell of triumph at having landed the thing at all?

Anyway, in the circumstances, we were relieved to walk away from the potential disaster. Until we beheld the bus which had been provided to take the press party on to Jamshedpur; an ancient thing, held together with string and tape. Anxiously, therefore, we asked the courier who was travelling with us how long the journey was likely to take. "Oh, two-and-a-half hours," he said.

They always say that. It took ten. (Whenever I tell this story, that produces a very satisfying gasp from the audience.)

We left the suburbs of Calcutta as dusk was falling and headed off into the hinterland of West Bengal on roads which only occasionally seemed to have much tarmac on them. The lights of the city were left behind as we rumbled on through the night.

At some stage, in the middle of nowhere, with not a light to be seen and many of us dozing uncomfortably, the bus juddered to a halt. Those of us who were awake peered through the windscreen and saw that a large tree trunk had been laid across the road. Then we became aware that the bus was surrounded by armed bandits, or dacoits as they are known in that part of the world. And now, being bright fellows, we thought, *We could be in a spot of bother here.*

We had our courier with us, who was knee-high to a grasshopper, but always claimed that he had royal Rajput blood in his veins, because his uncle, he said, was a maharaja. So he was the one we chose to send out to talk to the dacoits. And we closed the door firmly behind him.

There followed about ten minutes of animated negotiation at the roadside, while a bus full of journalists watched anxiously to see if our throats were about to be cut.

Eventually our man climbed back into the bus. The tree trunk was moved and the bandits melted away into the night. As we got moving again, we asked the question. "Raju, what did you say to them? How did you save our lives?"

He drew himself up to his full five-foot-nothing and said, "I told them to fuck off!"

I like to think it demonstrated the advantage of spending a bit of time with the British press.

Audience reaction to stories like that showed that entertaining rather than informing was perhaps our forte, so, in the years since, I have always been slightly surprised by audience members who approach us after a show saying, "That was very interesting."

Now we had five shows booked for June of the same year. Unfortunately, in this year of the Queen's diamond jubilee, our agent's booker had failed to spot the special jubilee weekend and had booked us into Swindon the day before the festivities were to start, and Dunstable the day after they were due to finish. We were proving slightly less of an attraction than the glorious Thames river pageant and the many other events. Tickets were not selling and so these first two shows were postponed.

The omens were still not looking good when our booking for the following weekend in Hastings was cancelled because the theatre had failed to sell many seats, though Blowers had warned me that this particular theatre had proved sticky in the past. We were beginning to wonder if we would ever do a show.

At last, on Saturday 16th June 2012, we set off for Bristol and our first professional performance together. It was a wet evening, but a fair crowd turned up at the converted St George's Church. We had decided that we should take the stage to the *Test Match Special* signature tune. Waiting in the wings for those first familiar beats of 'Soul Limbo', it was very gratifying and reassuring to hear a satisfied, "Aaaah…" of recognition from the audience.

To cap that, Blowers had long since discovered that for him to address an audience at the outset as "My dear old things" was to get them on his side. At the book signings in the crypt bar afterwards, they seemed encouragingly enthusiastic. We were up and running!

Then came another disappointment, with the next weekend's show scheduled for Neath being called off with fewer than fifty seats sold. The pity was that I had realised that this was the home town of our old friend, the late Alun Williams. So, in addition to the tale of his first broadcast, I had been trawling through all the other stories told of him. For instance, he used to recall meeting a man in the centre of Cardiff, who greeted him with, "Oh, Mr Williams, I seen you on the wireless often."

Now, with Blowers on duty to commentate on what was then a rare One Day International series drubbing of Australia in the middle of the English cricket season, I took the chance to take a break with my wife in that country (where the cricket defeat was barely being reported), returning just in time for our next tranche of theatre dates.

Birmingham Town Hall started this new run, a block of a building in the middle of the city, on the inner racetrack of a ring road. Like Bristol a month before, this was more meeting hall than theatre, but we had some friendly faces in the audience, including my daughter, Claire, with a couple of friends and the jovial presence of the former Warwickshire and England player John Jameson, and all seemed to enjoy themselves.

The next evening, a warm one in the western suburbs of London, we played our first proper theatre, in Richmond on Thames. Appropriately, I'm sure, there was a photograph of Laurence Olivier on the wall opposite Blowers' dressing room. In the style of one of the great masters of the stage, Henry had already announced that he had "played this theatre before", so I knocked on his door to indicate the picture and let him know that "dear Larry" must have been here, too.

Whatever magic the delightful place possessed, we had our best show yet – not a bad thing, as our agent, Neil O'Brien, was in the audience. We really began to feel that we had a pretty good thing going.

Ah, pride before – not quite a fall, but a much less satisfying evening. Three days later in Swindon. The Wyvern Theatre is in a rather prosaic concrete jungle and the messages on the screens in the foyer advertised us as *Memories of the Test Match Special*. Somehow the addition of that 'the' demonstrated that they had no idea what they had got.

It was a lesson we were to learn repeatedly. We knew we could put on an entertaining evening which audiences seemed to enjoy; we just needed the right publicity to haul them in. The best compliments we got were on the lines of, "I didn't really want to come, because I don't know anything about cricket, but I really enjoyed it!"

Blowers

I AM OFTEN ASKED – and all the more so since he announced his retirement from radio commentary in 2017 – when I first met Henry Blofeld. People expect a particular moment to have stuck in my mind. But it hasn't.

My first meeting with Christopher Martin-Jenkins I remember very clearly, because it was in the unlikely setting of Chelsea Football Club, where he was providing a match report on a game for which I was producing the commentary. (I can't remember the game, though.) I had heard plenty about the Sports News department's new recruit, so I was interested to meet him.

I know I had heard plenty about Henry Blofeld before I met him, too. He had made his BBC commentary debut at the end of the 1972 season on two of the matches in the first-ever series of One Day Internationals played in England. By that time I was in Munich to work on coverage of the Olympics, so I did not hear any of it. I was not to take the production reins of *Test Match Special* until the start of the following season, but I had been involved with the programme and had heard that this fellow had done a very good job in the West Indies at the start of the year.

The story of how that came about, we were eventually to include in our show. New Zealand were on their first tour of the Caribbean and Blowers had just about managed to put together enough commissions for newspaper writing work there to make it worth his while to follow the series. Indeed, his account of it is in the 1973 *Wisden Almanack*.

On the eve of the first first-class game, with Jamaica to take on the touring team at Sabina Park, Henry ran into the New Zealand radio commentator, Alan Richards, in their hotel. It was the first time they had met, but Alan asked if they might dine together and, during the meal, enquired if Blowers had ever done any radio commentary.

Now, he had done an audition commentary a couple of years earlier, but, despite being told that it was quite promising, he had been warned that opportunities were few and subsequently had heard nothing. So now, shrewdly sensing an opening, he said, "I've practically done nothing else!"

This was a lifesaver for Richards. Radio New Zealand had contacted the Caribbean Broadcasting Union before the tour, to agree that he could join their local commentary team in each territory for all the Tests and other island matches – a commentary that could then also be broadcast in New Zealand. So that morning, as he watched his team's practice session at the ground, he was not surprised to be approached by a gentleman giving him instructions about the next day's commentary.

He was a little more surprised a bit later, when another man approached him to ask, "You are Alan Richards? And you are OK to commentate with us tomorrow?"

Alan confirmed that that was what he had agreed to do and the man pointed to a box which seemed, to a slightly disorientated Richards, to be at the opposite end of the ground from the first one. He dismissed that as being part of the charming uncertainty of life in the West Indies until, later in the day, he discovered that there are, in every island, two competing radio stations: the one affiliated to the CBU and a rival commercial station, in this case Radio Jamaica (RJR). So he had agreed to commentate at the same time from opposite ends of the ground. And now he was appealing to Blowers for help.

The next morning, Alan introduced his new best friend to Winston Ridgarde of RJR as a celebrated English commentator. Henry commentated on the Jamaica v New Zealand game and his hosts were pleased enough to invite him to join them for the Test Match a week later. Other commercial stations round the Caribbean heard the commentaries and followed suit and Blowers became something of a star performer.

While the then head of radio outside broadcasts at the BBC, Robert Hudson, was unlikely to have heard any of those commentaries, he certainly heard about them. So, early in the English season, he suggested that Henry be sent out to a county match. The Whit weekend championship game between Essex and Warwickshire was chosen. Hudson was himself one of the best commentators on cricket, rugby and the great occasions of state. He could also spot potential and now he spotted that in H. C. Blofeld. Some more county cricket assignments followed and then the invitation to join the team for those two One Day Internationals.

As a rule for a successful career, being in the right place at the right time is not a bad starter.

As for Alan Richards, mention of him, when we told this tale on stage, prompted another story of a misunderstanding on a New Zealand tour. This time it was in Pakistan, where again his colleagues had contacted Radio Pakistan for Alan to join in a shared commentary for the series. Alan arrived at the ground on the first morning of the opening Test Match to be given a huge welcome and told how honoured they were to have him with them. Pakistan's lead commentator described the first twenty minutes' play and then effusively welcomed the esteemed Mr Alan Richards to the microphone.

Alan diffidently accepted the praise and commentated on the next twenty minutes in his usual matter-of-fact style. At the end of it he handed over to the next commentator, whose name had been written down for him. This gentleman gave another huge tribute to their guest commentator, before settling down to his task of twenty minutes' commentary – in Urdu.

Back in Wellington, panic set in, as technicians were jerked out of their lethargy by the unfamiliar language. But they could find no English-language commentary, and so had to resort to playing music – a policy they were forced to pursue for twenty minutes in every hour for the rest of the series.

Alan Richards, stalwart and dependable commentator that he was, was not overburdened with a sense of humour and failed to find either this, or his desperate recruitment of Blowers, amusing. Indeed, at the end of one New Zealand tour of England, he told me that I should put a curb on Brian Johnston's humour. Not advice that I took.

In March 1973, I was invited by Robert Hudson to become BBC Radio's cricket producer. One of the first events of my tenure was the annual cricket meeting in which all the regional outside broadcast producers – and there was one each from Birmingham, Bristol and Cardiff and two from Manchester (as far as I can remember, Glasgow and Belfast were not represented at the meeting) – met at a different venue each spring to decide on how cricket would be covered and, crucially, the make-up of the Test Match commentary teams. We even picked the first couple of months' worth of county championship matches to be covered on the Saturday sports programmes.

Brian Johnston had reached the compulsory BBC retirement age of sixty the previous year and so had left the staff and his post as cricket correspondent at the end of that 1972 season. No replacement had been appointed, though one of those at the meeting was keen on getting the job. That was one of the pair from Manchester, Don Mosey.

The situation made for a bit of tension as we assembled, though Hudson was keeping his powder dry on the subject.

The great John Arlott, who had commentated on every home Test since 1947, but had never got on with my predecessor, Michael Tuke-Hastings, and claimed never to have been certain that he was going to be employed from season to season, had now asked if he could only work on the radio for the first half of a day's play, so that he could devote the latter half to his writing for the *Guardian*. Some of his colleagues suggested that it might be that he was more concerned with devoting that period to wine consumption.

The new arrangement meant that an extra commentator could come in to take over his later shifts. In that season that role was filled alternately by Alan Gibson and Neil Durden-Smith. But in the final Test, Christopher Martin-Jenkins was brought in to make his debut. So far, no room for Blofeld, though for CMJ, in advance of England's winter tour of the West Indies, came the appointment as the BBC's second cricket correspondent – to the fury of Don Mosey.

At the spring cricket meeting of 1974, we again wrestled with the question of the 'relief' commentator to take over from Arlott, but I argued that it was not entirely fair on any commentator to have to join a team that was already in full flow halfway through the day. (That opinion might have been informed by the fact that, when it was his turn, Alan Gibson was inclined to spend the inactive first half of the day in the bar.) It would have been Bob Hudson who put forward the thought that it was time for Henry Blofeld to be tried. And so at last I was able to ring Blowers and offer the invitation for the first Test of that season – against India at Old Trafford.

In those days any outside broadcast was regarded as the production responsibility of the local producer. I might be the network cricket producer and as such would send the details of what was required to the regional office, but, unless invited, I would stay in the London studio for any event outside my 'patch' of London and the south-east. At the ground it was Don Mosey who was the producer for Blowers' debut *TMS* Test – and, incidentally, CMJ's second.

Our Indian expert summariser for that series, recruited by Robert Hudson, was the Maharaja of Baroda, who had managed a few Indian touring teams. When he arrived in England, I was called to Bob's office to meet him. Over cups of tea we set out what we expected of him during the three-Test series. As we were finishing our business, particularly conscious of India's abolishing of all titles, I asked the Maharaja how we should address him on the air.

He cast a lofty look at the ceiling. "I should be introduced as 'His Highness Lieutenant Colonel Fatehsingh Gaekwad, the former Maharaja of Baroda.'"

Looking over his shoulder, I could see Bob Hudson rolling his eyes. "Every time?" I asked.

"Oh, just the first two or three times," he said. "After that, 'Prince' will do."

So we called him 'Prince' throughout the series and a number of people thought we must have a dog in the commentary box.

The Maharaja was in the expert's seat, alternating with Trevor Bailey, as Blowers squeezed into the tiny commentary box alongside the Stretford End scoreboard at Old Trafford on 6th June 1974. His fellow commentators were John Arlott, Brian Johnston and Christopher Martin-Jenkins.

There was rain about and it interrupted play persistently. Interestingly, this was the first Test played in England in which play could be extended by up to an hour to make up time lost to the weather. While we were still in an era when prolonged breaks in play meant handing back to the studio for music to be played (indeed, one of my own early days of duty in the basement of Broadcasting House was greeted by soggy weather in the north, during which I ran through most of my stock of orchestral music selected by Radio 3 solely on account of its being out of any copyright or performance fees), there would still be some commentary box chat while conditions and plans were being assessed. This prospect did cause Blowers some concern.

He got away with it on the first day, but on the second he made the mistake of appearing in the box just as Johnners was looking round for someone to hand over to. But then he had an idea for a point he wanted to make. By his own modest admissions to our theatre audiences years later, he was eloquent, he was pertinent, he was interesting, he was entertaining – and he kept the peroration going for twelve-and-a-half minutes, looking neither to right nor left of him.

When at last he drew breath, he looked to his right, where a summariser or two – Trevor or the Prince, perhaps – should have been sitting. But the seat was empty. Nor was there anyone in Bill Frindall's usual seat to his left.

Then he spotted a note in Brian Johnston's unmistakable scrawl. *Keep going till 6.30, then hand back to the studio.* As Blowers himself would observe, he was being taught a lesson. This is a team game.

Blowers' next Test on commentary was at Headingley the following month, when Pakistan were England's opposition. There, Don Mosey finally had his wish granted to join the commentary team, though he also produced the outside broadcast, an arrangement he found very taxing. That had the effect that in the future I would be invited to invade the north region when he was commentating, to handle the production. I didn't actually have my passport stamped, but it came close.

In August at Lord's, I finally found myself producing Blowers on the ground for a Test in which Derek Underwood made the most of the effects of the weather to take thirteen wickets, but that weather had the final say in a drawn match.

Test Match Special is a family and we spend a lot of time in each other's pockets, particularly when it comes to touring. And I suppose, especially since the deaths of Christopher Martin-Jenkins and Bill Frindall, Blowers and I are now the pair with the longest memories of the programme. Indeed, I remember, as his retirement approached, Blowers would point out that he was the last on the team to have worked alongside John Arlott.

We have probably seen each other at our best and our worst. I certainly remember being less than delighted with him when he decided to overrun his commentary slot by nearly an hour to describe what looked likely to be an exciting finish to England's inaugural Test with Zimbabwe in Bulawayo. But I had my revenge a week later, when I detailed him to interview Robert Mugabe, when that gentleman visited the Test Match in Harare. His subsequent account of the President's halitosis made it sound almost literally like a poisoned chalice.

The time we have spent together made our on-stage relationship all the easier when it came to the ad-libbed moments, even when an interruption came with an intent of mischief.

- 3 -

Progression & Development

Having got into the swing of the *Memories of Test Match Special* shows in June and July of 2012, we now had a bit of an interruption. Sensibly, our agent had decided that running 'Blofeld and Baxter' against the London Olympics would be something of an uneven contest, but we reconvened for an autumn run of a dozen shows, which took us from Cornwall to North Yorkshire.

We were still at the point of remembering stories during the course of a show. I expect there must have been a visible sign of panic on the face of either of us when the other suddenly embarked on a "That reminds me…" and a totally new tale was related.

Two items of commentary history had survived from our first show: the ways in which the two giants of the commentary box, John Arlott and Brian Johnston, had started in broadcasting. We would make the point that Arlott was the best commentator, while Johnston had the greatest enduring influence on *Test Match Special.*

Arlott was a policeman who wrote poetry. At the end of the Second World War, he had sent some of his verse to John Betjeman, whom he had previously met, for his approval. Betjeman in turn had recommended Arlott to the BBC, who promptly engaged him as the literary producer in their Eastern Service. In 1946 India sent the first postwar cricket team to tour England, and the Eastern Service, whose target audience was in that part of the world, felt they should cover the tour. As it turned out, Arlott was the only member of their departmental staff who knew the first thing about cricket, so he was dispatched to report – and occasionally commentate – on the opening exchanges of the tour. The BBC's man in Delhi reported back to Bush House that Arlott's broadcasts had been so well received in India that he should keep doing them.

Meanwhile the domestic service, too, were impressed enough to take him into their Test Match commentary team to join the likes of Rex Alston and E. W. Swanton the following year. He was taken on with the ringing endorsement of the head of Outside Broadcasts: "You have a vulgar voice, but an interesting mind." With the right audiences, quick on the uptake, I could add, "Henry Blofeld, by contrast…" and need go no further. And, of course, Arlott's voice was his fortune, much as Blowers' own distinctive voice has been his.

A career that started with Eton, Oxford and the Brigade of Guards provided a distinct contrast with that of John Arlott. But that was Brian Johnston's life before the BBC. In our shows, Blowers would also tell how, before the war, Brian had been out to Brazil to supervise matters in the family coffee business – as one does. He had become very ill there, but, when war broke out, he was commissioned into the Grenadier Guards and indeed won an MC in the Guards Armoured Division's advance on Arnhem.

The one thing he did have in common with Arlott was that his post-war career was sparked by the good fortune of an earlier acquaintance. Lunching in the Guards Club in London one day, he ran into two well-known broadcasters he'd met during the war, Wynford Vaughan-Thomas and Stuart Macpherson. They asked him, as he seemed to be at a loose end, if he would be interested in joining the BBC. As Blowers would tell it, he replied, "Oh, I might as well do that as anything!"

The next morning, in Blowers' words, "As he was just tucking into his second boiled egg", he got a call to say that there seemed to be a vacancy in the Outside Broadcasts department. And the rest is history, though I would usually point out to our audiences that BBC recruitment policy has changed just a little since then.

Johnners' first broadcast was to commentate on the blowing up of a wartime German bomb that had been discovered in a lake in St James's Park. He took up his position on a nearby bridge, but a policeman told him it was far too dangerous there and he would have to move into "that building over there".

'That building over there' turned out to be a ladies' lavatory. So the great broadcasting career of Brian Johnston started with him standing on a loo seat, peering out of the window. And, being Johnners, of course he had to say, "I think I emerged looking a little flushed."

There was one Brian Johnston story which had always been a favourite of mine. Indeed, I had been using it in after-dinner speeches for years. When I mentioned it to Blowers, it turned out that he had been there for the moment. So we incorporated it into the show.

Early in 1968, England were in the West Indies under Colin Cowdrey's captaincy. England won that series one-nil, their only victory coming in Trinidad in the fourth Test. The day before that match, Henry and Brian found themselves independently at the morning practice session; Blowers for a couple of newspapers and Johnners as BBC correspondent. They agreed to share a taxi back to the hotel.

Now, the rumour was around that one of the press party had acquired an extremely attractive girlfriend – and Trinidad is littered with some exceptionally beautiful women. So far, none of the other journalists had seen this one, though. Arriving back at the colonial-style hotel, Johnners and Blowers could see, at the far end of the open bar, their colleague with this vision of pulchritude. Brian made a beeline for the couple, leading the way between the wicker armchairs. The man knew he had been run to earth, so he decided to make a brave face of it.

"Brian," he said, "I don't think you've met Annette. Annette, this is Brian."

"Oh," said Johnners. "Every time you said you were going to have a net, I thought you were going to practise cricket."

After our break for the 2012 Olympics, we returned at an unusual-looking venue, the Huntingdon Hall in Worcester.

It is a deconsecrated Methodist church and we took the stage with a pulpit at our backs and an inscription which suggested that God had his eye on us – and not necessarily in a benevolent way.

One of our continuing problems with the stage set was highlighted by the fact that we always required a pair of armchairs, to create the illusion of the two old buffers in their club. Ideally, to get the right sort of chairs, of course, we should have been taking them around with us, but we were just travelling in our own cars, not a van. So the agent's notice of what we required, sent to each theatre in advance – known as the 'rider' – would include these armchairs. The trouble was that some theatres would not look at the rider in advance (some even not at all) and others might look at it, shrug and say to themselves, "Well, we haven't got anything like that" and not give it another thought.

It has to be said that there were some theatres that went to great lengths to help. The Hall for Cornwall in Truro, for instance, a month after this, struck a deal with a nearby hotel to borrow two fine chairs from their foyer, which they were told they could have after 6pm, by which time most people had checked in. As soon as the show finished they were the first items off the stage to be returned to the hotel.

In Worcester, it seemed, welcoming as they were, with meal vouchers for their cafe, the rider had not been closely studied. We were offered a pair of upright chairs from the auditorium, which only served to enhance the impression of a prayer meeting. So we searched the building and found two office-desk chairs with arms, which did rather better.

Nor was Huntingdon Hall the only venue we would have to search for furniture. Sometime later, in Lancaster, a chaise longue from a bar three floors up had to be pressed into service and manoeuvred down the precipitous stairs. But the highlight was the pair of armchairs borrowed from the next-door pub landlord's sitting room in Chipping Norton, which took great ingenuity and effort from most of his clientele to wrestle down a narrow staircase and out through the public bar.

One item of the set which did travel with us and had been there from the start, was a small basket for written questions, to which we devoted the last fifteen to twenty minutes of the show. For some time Henry had been using the technique in his one-man show. It is more controllable than having questions shouted out from the audience. There were usually some favourite topics. Geoffrey Boycott would be a popular one, and during those early days Kevin Pietersen was another that got Blowers coming in off his long run. I do remember that at Worcester there was another familiar question: "Which is your favourite county cricket ground?"

It sounded a loaded question to me, but Blowers stroked his chin to ponder, so I interjected, "Blowers, remember where we are!" And suddenly he recalled the view across the Severn from New Road to the cathedral.

The great thing about written questions was being able to leave out or adjust the dull or awkward ones to our advantage. They might easily prompt a fresh story, and in the early days it was often a reminder for one or other of us of a tale we had not yet told.

One evening we had a particularly unimaginative collection emerging from the basket, so, knowing that it would produce a favourite five-minute story which could provide a good finish, I threw in, "Blowers, we've been asked about cake."

The response was slightly delayed. "Cake? Oh, cake!" he said, picking up enthusiasm as he recognised his cue.

It is a two-handed story, which Blowers starts with the background to the extensive commentary box consumption of cakes. It all started in the '70s, when "a lovely lady – I'm sure she must have been a lovely lady" sent Brian Johnston a cake. Being well brought up, Johnners thanked her on the air and so the next day two more cakes were sent in. And so it went on. The more Brian mentioned the cakes, the more turned up.

"But," Blowers would say, "I want to tell you about a very special cake.

"In 2001, Steve Waugh's Australians were in England and on the Friday of the Lord's Test, the Queen decided to come down and see an hour of play, take tea in the Committee Room and meet the teams. And the palace decreed that she should bring with her a very special fruit cake to present to us. Actually, I don't think it came with her in the Rolls, but went on ahead with a motor-bicycle escort. I believe the cake was a bit miffed about that, but then there aren't many fruit cakes that get a motor-bicycle escort."

At that point I would sometimes try to intervene with a, "Well, you should know, Blowers—", but he was usually in too good a flow either to hear or care.

He would go on to tell how, in the tea interval, five of us – he and I, Christopher Martin-Jenkins, Jonathan Agnew and Bill Frindall – fought our way round to the pavilion. In fact, it was raining, so the space under the Mound Stand, our chosen route, was especially crowded, as was the pavilion itself, because, in the rain, the teams' presentation to the Queen had had to be done in the Committee Room, rather than the usual setting on the grass in front. So MCC members were pressed into every nook and cranny to get a view of proceedings through the glass doors. There was a moment when I really thought we could not possibly make it. But we did.

At this point in the narrative Blowers would hand the tale to me, as he would say, "Backers, as our venerable producer, was the first to meet Her Majesty.'"

As she handed me this splendid Dundee cake on a silver salver, she gave me a rather quizzical look, as if she didn't quite trust the brief she'd been given.

"They tell me people give you cake," she said.

I confirmed that this was the case and then introduced her down the line of the others (though I think they knew who she was).

Blowers would now take up his story again. "When she came to me, looking at the rain outside, she said, 'You must find it so awfully difficult to keep going when there's nothing happening.'

"And I said, 'Well, you know, Your Majesty, when it rains we do try to keep going and we talk about anything and everything and many of our listeners write in to tell us how much better we are when there's nothing going on.'

"I thought that might bring a smile or even a chuckle to the lips of the head of the House of Windsor. I got that badly wrong. She looked as mournful as Fred Basset on a particularly bad day and said, 'Oh, how dreadfully sad.'"

He would then tell of Aggers' encounter with the Queen and how he leapt in with, "Did you make it yourself, ma'am?"

"Which," as Blowers would say, "was as bad a case of *lèse-majesté* as any I've heard. And if he had done that with the first Queen Elizabeth, he'd have ended up in the Tower of London in double-quick time. But she was very good. She just said, 'No, but it was made under strict personal supervision.'"

He would then hand the telling back to me, because, having met all of us, she looked at the group and asked me, "If you're all here, how are you staying on the air?"

I thought of our ABC colleague, Tim Lane, manfully holding the fort in the commentary box and said, "Well, ma'am, we have an Australian."

She said, "Oh. They're very useful, aren't they?"

After that first use of the story in our question session, back in the dressing room, Blowers said, "Thank goodness we had that question about the cake!"

"We didn't," I said. But after that we decided to include this in future as our final question, whether it had been asked or not, thus ensuring a strong finish.

- 4 -

The Spirit of CMJ

BY THE AUTUMN TOUR of 2012, which had started only three months after our first show, we had developed a fairly settled routine, though either of us was still likely to sling in an unexpected googly, which just kept us on our toes.

On a pleasant early-September Saturday afternoon, I drove to Bury St Edmunds, a town I had not visited for many years. So, as I was rather early for setting the stage at the delightful Theatre Royal, I wandered downtown and chose a cafe in the sunshine, opposite the ancient abbey gateway. Tea and a scone were going down happily and progress was being made with the newspaper crossword, when my phone rang. It was Blowers – of course.

"Backers, I've done something rather stupid, I'm afraid." He had, it transpired, just filled his diesel car with petrol. The only good news was that he had realised his mistake before restarting the engine. The RAC man could not get to him in time for him to be able to get to the theatre, so he had asked the petrol station attendant if he could leave the car there overnight and then rung an old friend, Johnny Wheeler of the wine merchant Lay & Wheeler, to beg a lift and a bed for the night.

As I returned to get organised in the splendid surroundings of the restored Regency theatre, I was reminded of our old friend and colleague Christopher Martin-Jenkins, for whom such a crisis as Blowers was currently involved in would have been business as usual.

Blowers arrived just in time to avoid a delayed curtain-up, but early in the show I introduced a favourite tale of CMJ, who had a tremendous reputation for lateness. Indeed, we always insisted that he might never have seen the first ball of a match. It was possible, we thought, that he did not know that there was a first ball of a match. It was just one of those things that was already going on when you got there.

At a One Day International at the Oval, just before the first ball was bowled, my phone rang and it was him. "You're always telling me I'm late," he said, and I agreed. "Well, I want you to know that today I was early."

I inspected not a very large commentary box and could see no sign of his having arrived.

"There's only one problem," he explained. "I went to Lord's."

To his regret, his time as BBC cricket correspondent came before correspondents had broadcasting points installed in their houses so that they could instantly report on news items in their area of expertise. In his day, he had to make the journey – not too far – from his Sussex home into Horsham, where there was a BBC self-operated studio. Unfortunately, he had discovered the world record time for this journey with no traffic, all the lights on green, a following wind, and a parking space in the street immediately outside. That time was what he allowed every time, so that, whenever he was required to do a 'live' piece for the evening *Sports Desk*, I was always put on standby in case he did not make it. I think I was used more often than he was.

Sadly, two months after this Bury St Edmunds show, I saw CMJ for what turned out to be the last time. He was in the final stages of the cruel and unforgiving cancer which would take his life within ten months of its diagnosis.

When we got going with the show again the following year, barely a month after his death, we would pay tribute to his talent as a model for any aspiring commentator. At the microphone he was generally completely organised, but it was, as we would reflect on stage, the only organised part of his life. The rest was utter chaos. I always thought that maybe his splendid memorial service in a packed St Paul's might have started even more appropriately with the clock chiming eleven, followed by an elaborate oath along the lines of his favourite "Fotheringay Thomas!" or "Fishcakes and buttercup pie!", a chair scraping back, a slamming door and running footsteps. The prelude, in other words, to most of his commentaries.

Technology was always a mystery to him and why he wore a watch we never discovered. Not only was he late for every commentary stint (whoever was preceding him at the microphone would look round to see who was next and, finding no one there, would know it was meant to be Christopher), but he would also habitually overrun his time. He shared with Brian Johnston a preference for plain food. This aspect of his life could make tours of India something of a trial. Calcutta, it seemed, was his particular nemesis.

At the 1987 World Cup Final at Eden Gardens, Calcutta, I was surprised when he rose from the commentary desk uncharacteristically early and, as he shot past me in the back of the box, announced, "I'm going back to the hotel for a comfortable one!"

From Eden Gardens there stretches a half-mile or so of park, the Maidan, through to the busy street, Chowringhee, and our usual hotel, the Oberoi Grand. From the back of the stand CMJ could be seen trying to hurry back to safety, accelerating – but only from the knees downwards. As Blowers would usually add, "He looked like Hercule Poirot, as portrayed by David Suchet." But, we reassured our audiences, he made it.

In the press box he became known as 'the Major'. It was after the character in Fawlty Towers and was, I believe, a rank conferred on him by Mike Selvey, after he arrived one day with the announcement, "I see Hampshire won."

Echoing the scene from the programme, Selvey responded, like Basil Fawlty, "Did it, Major?"

But CMJ nearly floored Selve on the air one day when he attempted some Cockney rhyming slang of his own invention. "I've gone in the Conrad," he proclaimed.

Mike had to think of Conrads. Hilton came to mind and Joseph Conrad, but neither seemed to work and unfortunately one name did keep presenting itself to him –

the former West Indian opening batsman, Conrad Hunte. He kept trying to suppress the thought, not least because it was the unlikeliest of options. Eventually, he had to ask.

With wide-eyed innocence CMJ said, "Conrad Black. I've got a bad back."

The tale of him trying and failing to get through to the *Times* sports desk from Jamaica on his mobile phone has been often told and we spun that one out. As he failed to get through, the instrument, as with all equipment that let Christopher down, was bashed with impotent fury, before it was pointed out to him that this was the television remote control from his hotel room.

Blowers placed that story on a drive from Montego Bay to Kingston, for which he recommended a stop at the Blue Mountain Inn where, he insisted, "The banana flambé is to die for!" Unfortunately, during one show in Nottingham, he got his wording slightly wrong and called it 'Jamaica Inn'.

At the time the BBC were showing a dramatised version of Daphne du Maurier's novel of the same name, which was coming under fire for a lack of clarity of dialogue, so I asked if the people there were all mumbling. The audience enjoyed the joke, but it was obvious to all of us that Blowers, not having seen the show, had no idea what we were going on about. We somehow got over the hiatus.

On that same West Indies tour, while pasting cuttings into his notebook, CMJ was mystified that the music he was listening to on his Walkman went silent. After more impact technology being applied, he realised that he had cut through his headphone cable.

Even that was not the end of his Caribbean troubles. Golf was a hugely important part of his life and in Barbados he got the chance to play the prestigious Sandy Lane course. For the occasion he borrowed from an acquaintance a very superior set of clubs, promising their safe return. Coming off the eighteenth green, he was running late for his next appointment. He always was. He slung the borrowed set of clubs in the back of his hired Mini Moke, like an ashtray on wheels, and set off at breakneck speed through the streets of Bridgetown, back to his hotel, taking every bend nearly on two wheels and completely unaware of the fact that, as he took each corner, another club would take flight out of his bag.

He arrived back at his hotel and retrieved the golf bag from the back of the Moke, astonished to find it empty. Those who witnessed this said that the double take he did was quite theatrical and was followed by him turning the bag upside down and shaking it. Unsurprisingly, no clubs fell out. He then beat the empty bag against the wretched car in his impotent fury. More reminders of Basil Fawlty.

The next day he was on the air on Voice of Barbados from the cricket and appealed for the return of the clubs by anyone who might have found them. I regret to say that not a single club was handed in.

Over the next year many legends of the great Christopher Martin-Jenkins would be added to our repertoire. Indeed, a cricket club member approached us with one. This man had been at an after-dinner speech given by Christopher at the Yellowhammers Cricket Club in Kent. He started with a golf-related story and then followed it with another on the same subject. When the third tale was also about golf, his audience were a little surprised. Then he suddenly stopped dead. "Oh, sorry," he said, "I've picked up the wrong notes. Just a minute." And with that he shot out to his car to retrieve the right speech notes and began again.

My favourite, which we also used, was of a time when he was doing an after-dinner speech in Yorkshire and his eye kept falling on two old men who would not laugh or even crack a smile. And Christopher was a very funny speaker. As he sat down he heard one of these old boys say to the other, "What do you make of t'speaker, then?"

"All right," said his friend. "If yer like laffing."

Thus the spirit of CMJ stayed with us.

Such are the inherent contrasts of a theatre tour that our next venue, a couple of days after Bury St Edmunds, was at Salford Quays, just across the water from the new BBC centre of 'Media City'. This was where my old BBC department had now been deposited, so I was grateful to Henry Moeran, *TMS*'s new assistant producer, for showing me round. It did not make me any more convinced that the BBC had made the right decision.

Two other venues stood out in that autumn tour. There was a Friday five o'clock show at the Oxford Playhouse, for which we had to abbreviate our usual show to fit into a slot before the evening performance of *Noises Off*, starring Liza Goddard and Gareth Hale. Such was the rush to clear the theatre afterwards that, I realised when I was unloading the car at home, I left our little bit of carpet behind. It transpired when I went to fetch it next day that *Noises Off* had been performed, for one night only, over my old carpet, apparently without the cast noticing.

From there it was Cornwall, followed a day or two later by North Yorkshire. In Richmond, we were genuinely charmed by the Georgian Theatre Royal, where we did two consecutive sell-out nights. Founded in 1788 (but out of action for a 115-year period before 1963), it claims to be the oldest working theatre in its original form. We found that we were performing to an audience for the most part on bench seats in the stalls, but also filling the boxes, two of which were effectively just beside us on the stage.

We were to return to Richmond four years later, when we recorded one notable triumph. An American couple had apparently come into the foyer about half an hour before the show, saying that it had always been their desire to see this historic theatre. The manager told them that unfortunately they couldn't really look round, because a performance was about to start. He also told them that, as it was based on cricket, they probably wouldn't understand it. But so determined were they to see the theatre that they bought tickets. Telling us about this after the show, the manager said, "The extraordinary thing is, they came back for the second half!"

Proof that the American colonies are not necessarily entirely lost.

- 5 -

Valeria

NOT LONG BEFORE HIS seventieth birthday in 2009, while having lunch in a Chelsea restaurant, Blowers met an attractive lady of Italian origin. He charmed her enough that the unusual invitation, "Do come and see me at the Albert Hall", was accepted. The lady in question – Valeria – thought he must be a conductor or something like that. I don't think she considered the possibility of an ageing rock star.

In fact he was taking over the Royal Albert Hall for one night, some weeks in advance of the event, to celebrate that milestone birthday. The first half of the evening's entertainment, which drew a satisfying crowd, was essentially the one-man show Blowers had been doing. The second half was hosted by Jonathan Agnew, who, after interviewing the great man himself, introduced a succession of old friends and colleagues who were encouraged to say a few words of appreciation and maybe tell a relevant story.

He started with Henry's brother, Sir John Blofeld, the retired high court judge and followed with an eclectic mix which included Sir Tom Courtney, Christine Hamilton, the former England batsman Peter Richardson, the former *Times* cricket correspondent John Woodcock and a stellar performance from Stephen Fry.

When my own turn came, I plumped for a story that would occasionally make it into our show in future years. It came from Trent Bridge in 1994. For the Test Match against South Africa our commentary position had been moved into the newly opened Radcliffe Road Stand, directly opposite our old box slung on the front of the pavilion, which had been a favourite of commentators because of its intimacy with the game, but which had been a producer's nightmare because it was so small. Now, of course, we had a completely different view, looking back at the pavilion.

Blowers was in his element, freshly restored to the *TMS* team after a few years' sojourn with Sky TV. Not only could he describe that Victorian pavilion that was the backdrop for the action, but – glory be – he could see the buses going down the road into West Bridgford. Then he spotted in the distance a church on a hill. "Rather a good-looking church," he declared. On the second day, he spied a column of smoke appearing to rise from the churchyard. "Oh, look," he cried, "the vicar must be having a barbecue! What a good chap the vicar must be. So good to his parishioners."

In double-quick time two members of the Nottinghamshire committee arrived in our box to inform us that the subject of Blowers' joy was the Wilford Hill Crematorium.

On that night at the Albert Hall, Aggers had been a little anxious about how this procession of guests was going to work and I must confess that I may have added to his anxiety when I advised him that the long gap between the afternoon rehearsal and show time had provided some with plenty of opportunity to appreciate the supply of wine in the green room.

We were a motley crew, and what Valeria made of it all from the auditorium I can only imagine. She must have been slightly bemused, but suffice to say that by the time I next worked with Henry the following summer, doing commentary on a private Twenty20 tournament, he and Valeria were an item. Four years after that, I was delighted to be at their splendidly sociable wedding at Langar Hall in Nottinghamshire, an occasion which spread over three days and had elements which reminded me of an Agatha Christie country house murder mystery. Though, as far as I know, no one was struck down by a length of lead piping in the library.

In the meantime, Valeria had become an indispensable part of the support for the Blofeld and Baxter show. Her life in the fashion industry had given her an acute eye for the way things looked on stage and gradually we added to our set. A red rug was followed by an arrangement of artificial flowers. She was very good at finding other plant life around theatre foyers, which would then make its way onto the stage. Often a dull-looking stool that might have been requisitioned as a side table or plant stand would be transformed by the draping of the exotic wrap she had been wearing round her shoulders.

Inspired by this, gradually our originally rather austere stage set became more welcoming and comfortable. I remember particularly the Maddermarket in Norwich, where they embraced the idea of the two old gents in their club by producing a fireplace from their stores. It was just a mantlepiece with the two supporting side mouldings and a black void in the middle. Valeria swiftly found a vase of flowers to fill the space and suddenly it looked like home.

I acquired first one and then a second artificial palm to loom over the backs of our chairs. They had to put up with the indignity and perpetual leaf loss of being unceremoniously shoved in and out of my car. Then the picture was complete when, in a local charity shop, I found a standard lamp, which, with a bit of surgery involving gaffer tape, glue and Blu Tack, added to the cosiness.

The most obvious difference that Valeria's arrival made to Henry's life – apart from a general jauntiness in his step, of course – was to the increased colourfulness of his clothing. Now, Blowers was certainly not a dull dresser before, though I do remember a period early on when he seemed to reckon that Test Matches in the capital required a formal suit, while those in the provinces demanded little more than some might don for a day's fishing or shooting. Then came a few more adventurous jackets. I particularly remember one coat which appeared to have been cut from the same yellow-and-large-check cloth as Rupert the Bear's trousers.

But with Valeria's arrival, any previous inhibitions (and, to be frank, there had been few) were cast aside for the adoption of pink, lime green or orange, sometimes all at the same time. Just before one show we did in Scarborough, Blowers emerged to ask the opinion of my daughter, Claire, who was standing in for Valeria for the day, about his choice of outfit. Rather drily, she said, "A little citrus, I think, Blowers."

Front of house, the great service that Valeria did us both was to man a merchandise stall. There were books we had written, mugs with our own ugly mugs on them, and sometimes Blowers' own-label wine. Valeria handled our public with a rare charm and tact, and with that, who could resist buying?

I have no doubt at all that she has been very good for Henry and has entered into a world that must have been previously totally alien to her. I have even seen her watching cricket! I think she may have found that, whatever you might think of the game itself, cricketers are, by and large, pretty decent people.

- 6 -

Edinburgh

At the beginning of 2013, Blowers had said to me that we had been scheduled to do the show for a three-week run at the Edinburgh Festival Fringe. My first reaction was probably a bit sceptical as to whether it would actually happen. My only experience of the Edinburgh Festival had been as a child being taken to the Military Tattoo and then later being walked up the castle esplanade by my father, who, as a soldier himself, was explaining the difficulties of the performance I had seen on that sloping, rough arena. That apart, the word in the family had always been to avoid Edinburgh during the festival at all costs. Now I was to find the atmosphere utterly addictive.

As August approached, it was becoming clear that we really were going to do this. Another two dozen shows between February and July had honed our routine, but now we found that we would have to do a tight one-hour show and there were fines for any overruns. It wasn't until we got there that I realised why this had to be done. Most of the time, there was only half an hour between performances, so it was essential not to eat into this time for resetting the stage before and after your own slot.

We found it quite a pressure to be sure of our timing, which had previously, in a two-hour show with an interval, been quite relaxed. There would be no questions plucked from the basket, which we had been using as a bit of a cushion on the timing issue. We set a point in the routine which we had to reach with fifteen minutes left and agreed on what cuts we would make on the hoof if we were overrunning. Audience reaction, of course, could be a factor in this timing.

Blowers had performed at the Fringe before, doing a handful of shows with the antiques expert John Bly. He discovered that he had barely scratched the surface of what was needed. However, that experience had at least unearthed a wonderfully positioned and supremely comfortable bed-and-breakfast establishment in the Murrayfield area, high above Leith Water as it winds its way round the New Town of Edinburgh. Its proprietors were to become good friends of ours.

Our agent, Neil O'Brien, was not an Edinburgh Fringe expert, and Blowers' previous experience of it had been too brief to form any expertise himself, so we plunged into the unknown as complete innocents. Our venue was one of the many theatre spaces in the Pleasance Courtyard, grandly titled the Pleasance Forth. It was a medium-sized hall on the top floor of a building that housed the university gym and converting to a two-hundred-seat theatre for the festival made it one of the larger venues. (Some, after all, are barely more than a standard-sized room.)

The Pleasance Courtyard is a splendid complex of mostly old buildings round, in effect, three courtyards, and taking its name from the road it is on – the Pleasance. (Fans of Ian Rankin's books might remember that Inspector Rebus's St Leonards Police Station is just down the road.) Finding my way there across the city provided my satnav with a fine challenge, as the centre was being dug up for the prolonged works to install the new tramlines, so that turns demanded by the disembodied voice often proved impossible. (The tram works was a topic guaranteed to raise a groan from any locals.)

On the first morning visit to reconnoitre and drop off the necessary props for the set, I was in total ignorance of any parking possibilities and so quickly managed to fall expensively foul of the eager and rapacious traffic wardens. Neil O'Brien had dispatched one of his staff with the sole purpose of securing a pair of armchairs for our stage on loan from the university. He stayed to witness our first preview show that evening before he returned to London, to reappear in three weeks to restore the chairs whence they came.

I think we were both quite nervous about this first show, with the changes we had had to make to satisfy the critical timing issue. As it turned out, the act we were following, the comedian Nick Helm, had apparently fewer worries about timing. That first day he overran by twenty minutes and subsequently averaged being about ten minutes late for the rest of the run. The crew running the theatre were splendid and very friendly and helpful and always tried to make up the delay between shows as best they could, striking Helm's set before the audience were out and quickly getting our chairs, rug, plants and lamp into place. Late as he might finish, we were rarely anything like as delayed starting.

After the first rather rushed, but reasonably successful, outing, I asked the stage manager if they could put a bit of music on as the audience were coming in. "You provide it and we'll play it," was the response. So I dug through the CDs in my car to try to find something appropriate.

What no one had told us was that we were meant to have accreditation passes, or that two large boxes of promotional fliers had been delivered to the small ticket office at the front of the complex. It was only after two or three days that I became aware of them when my head was bitten off by someone behind the desk who was fed up with them being in the way. On advice, we spent a slightly embarrassing morning handing these fliers out in George Street. We were to get rather better at doing that with experience.

I don't think I had ever appreciated the sheer scale of the Fringe, which now dwarfs the original festival itself. With so many thousands of shows on, it is crucial to make people aware that you are there at all. Neil O'Brien had engaged a publicist for us quite late in the day and we met him just before our second show, which he came to see. He did raise interest from various newspapers, which involved several phone interviews for Blowers. Also, the teenage daughter of a friend of Valeria's decided that we needed our own Blofeld and Baxter Facebook page and promptly set it up for us.

On our second morning, Henry, Valeria and I walked alongside the Water of Leith to the cosmopolitan suburb of Stockbridge. During lunch in a restaurant there, Henry, as ever glued to his phone, exclaimed loudly, "Oh, someone's just tweeted that he's sitting near Henry Blofeld in a cafe in Edinburgh!"

A hugely embarrassed man at the next table looked round rather sheepishly.

We had included one completely new story for this show, an event which had happened in the commentary box at Trent Bridge only a few weeks before. During the previous winter an Irish duo called the Duckworth Lewis Method had been putting together an album called *Sticky Wickets*. The first track was called *It's Just Not Cricket* and as Blowers would put it in his telling of the tale, they decided it needed a bit of rapping. So, finding that neither Jay-Z nor Snoop Dogg was available, they went for the next best thing, which was, of course, H. Blofeld.

They called the Blofeld household to invite him to do some rapping, to which he replied that he wasn't much good at it and, come Christmas, he left that sort of thing to Valeria. They explained that it wasn't that sort of rapping and engaged him to come to a studio in what he described as "the dodgy end of Islington". There, he had, when prompted, interspersed their lively song with expressions such as 'My dear old thing', 'That won't do at all', 'Calypso collapso', 'How perfectly dreadful' and, of course, 'It's just not cricket'.

The CD was released and had some success, so that, for the first Test of the Ashes series that summer, the group came to Trent Bridge to appear in a lunch interval on *Test Match Special*. The engineers set them up in the commentary box during lunch and Blowers reprised his 'rapping' role. After the interval he was the first commentator on duty, alongside Phil Tufnell. He enjoyed being on with Tuffers, though he claimed that people were complaining that they could not tell their voices apart.

Inevitably, with the fast bowlers operating, the conversation between deliveries was of the musical interval. After a bit of cheery banter, Blowers decided it was time to move on and thought he would draw a line under the topic by declaring, "Yes, the Duckworth Lewis Method and Blowers!"

He was surprised to see Phil Tufnell turn away and put his head between his knees. On the other side of him the scorer, Malcolm Ashton, dropped his pen noisily and devoted some time scrabbling around on the floor to find it. Behind him, the producer, Adam Mountford, gave a loud guffaw. Henry was puzzled.

He was also alone, because his next attempt to get Tuffers to offer a comment on the cricket was greeted with, "Sorry, Blowers, I'm overcome with emotion" as he returned to fits of giggles.

Blowers managed to finish the commentary stint and, as he rose after handing on to Jim Maxwell, the assistant producer, Henry Moeran asked him if he knew what he'd said. "Yes," he said, "the Duckworth Lewis Method and Blowers."

"It didn't quite come out like that," said the younger Henry, and offered him some headphones to hear the recording.

What Blowers heard there was the declaration, "Yes, the Duckworth Lewis Method and – Blow Job!"

As he would tell our audiences, "I simply don't know where that came from. I can promise you that at that moment nothing was further from my mind."

After we had first decided to include the telling of this story in our show, we went for dinner to a packed restaurant in George Street. As we were taking our seats, Blowers said, rather too loudly, "I thought the 'Blow Job' went well tonight!" Several startled diners looked round in alarm.

Audiences continued to build as the days went by and in our last week we were coming close to full houses – something of a triumph for a Fringe show. But during the run we had begun talking to an acquaintance of Blowers' who, amongst other things, ran the comedy awards at the Fringe. She – Emma Brünjes – was an expert on how the festival (and, indeed, all the world of theatre) worked and, after a couple of meetings with her, it became clear that she might be very good for us and the future development of our show. We were about to change agents.

Also, intriguingly, a producer from an independent production company, Jonathan Harvey from Hat Trick, had come to see the show and suggested that we might be able to offer a version of it to Radio 4. Obviously that was an exciting prospect, though I could think of a couple of stories that might have to be cleaned up or dropped for that audience. We waited to see what might come of that.

Beyond the Fringe

Glowing with what had felt like a successful time in Edinburgh in August 2013, we plunged straight into a busy autumn tour, with seventeen shows all over the country in the space of six weeks.

Shortly before we started on it came the news of the death of an old friend and colleague of ours, the Welsh wizard of a rugby fly half of the 1950s, Cliff Morgan. He had gone on to be a broadcaster, sports editor, and head of both radio and television sports departments at the BBC, and his departure, we felt, warranted a story or two from the stage, particularly as one of our first shows of this run would be just across the border in Monmouth.

After recalling that one of his favourite expressions of surprise was always, "Well, shag my dog!", though admitting that I never met this unfortunate pooch, I would embark on a tale at one time beloved by broadcasters.

It happened in the early days of 1975, when England's cricketers were being battered by Messrs Lillee and

Thomson in the fourth Test in Sydney. *Test Match Special* in those days would only take commentary on the final session of the day's play – usually from 5–7am GMT, with telephone reports from Christopher Martin-Jenkins for Radio 2 through the night and for Radio 4 news in the mornings.

Brian Johnston had hosted *TMS* for the first three Tests, before going out to Australia to see the last three of the six-match series himself. He had already witnessed one near crisis on Boxing Day morning when, at ten to five, my studio manager had not put in an appearance. I knew who was scheduled on, a famously laid-back character, but one of the best and most accomplished and reliable technical operators there was, so I was not too worried. The Broadcasting House control room offered me the line from Melbourne, which I was just about technically competent enough to accept. I even managed to have a few exchanges of Christmas cheer with the former Australian captain Lindsay Hassett, who was already at the microphone after the tea break.

Johnners, on the talkback from the studio, could see that I was still alone on the other side of the glass and that it was I who was lacing up the tape to play the opening signature tune. "Everything all right, old man?" he asked.

I reassured him, before putting in a call to the studio managers' common room. There are not too many people hanging around there at 5am on Boxing Day, but I was lucky and someone came in to help me out, just as we were going on the air. The missing man, as we had predicted he would, strolled in, apparently unconcerned, an hour later.

He admitted that, though he had got up in good time, he had then fallen asleep in his chair as he drank his first cup of tea.

With Brian's departure Down Under, I needed someone else to be the studio presenter for the last three Tests. I could not do it myself, because I was always having to pop off to other studios to put them in touch with CMJ on the phone. The man I engaged was then our principal athletics commentator, Norman Cuddeford. Norman had also done plenty of county cricket commentaries and was a regular at Wimbledon.

Meanwhile, the editor of Radio 4's *Today* programme had suggested to me that he was not very happy with the line quality and possible unreliability of our telephone reports from CMJ in the programme's sports slots. They were also quite dangerously close to the Radio 2 updates on the half-hour. He asked me for any alternative suggestions.

I said that I did have a presenter in the *TMS* studio who would be completely up to date with goings-on in the match, and our studio was very close to *Today*'s. He could quickly nip up the stairs to give the latest news and I would cover any risk of the line going down while he was away. "That's great," the editor said. "What can possibly go wrong with that?"

The first day of the fourth Test arrived, and with it Norman Cuddeford, immaculate in a three-piece suit at five in the morning. As the 6.25 *Today* sports desk approached, I dispatched him to the relevant studio to do his report. He was met in the corridor by the morning's sports presenter, the former Scottish rugby international

Chris Rea, who once again ran through what they were going to be doing. Then they quietly slipped in to take their seats side by side at the studio table. It was not long before Desmond Lynam, who that day was presenting *Today* with John Timpson, said, "Now it's time for the sport, with Chris Rea."

Chris started, "We've got some football news to come and, of course, our racing tips, but first let's catch up with the fourth Test in Australia, and Norman Cuddeford can bring us up to date with England's progress in Sydney, can't you, Norman?"

Now, Norman was an experienced radio broadcaster and one of the things that we all know is that when you go into a studio the first thing they ask you to do is to give some voice level for the technicians to set their microphones. One usually comes up with something silly, like whatever you had for breakfast, just to make any sort of noise. However, in a studio that is on the air live for three hours, this is not going to be possible. That had not dawned on Norman.

So, to Chris's request to "bring us up to date", with his head down in his notebook he replied, "No, I'm frightfully sorry, I can't."

What followed was muted pandemonium. John Timpson put his head between his knees; Desmond Lynam tried to leave the studio, but forgot to take his headphones off and almost throttled himself; Chris Rea was making gathering motions with his hands while his mouth movements imitated a goldfish. Through the glass, the very experienced studio manager was opening every fader she could find, on the basis that there must be something here, mustn't there?

The only person who was totally unconcerned was Norman, still studying his notebook, until he looked up to say, "Was that all right?"

Chris recovered enough to tell him that it wasn't and asked again for the update.

My next encounter with the *Today* editor was less friendly. "That must never happen again," he said, as if I was plotting to undermine his programme yet further.

Norman, meanwhile, had returned to the *TMS* studio to suggest to me that maybe he should go later to apologise to the sports editor, who would be taking over as head of the department in a few weeks and was none other than Cliff Morgan. "Do you think it might be a good idea if I went to see old Cliffie?" he asked.

I wasn't sure, but was conscious that, with the Canadian Olympics approaching, Norman was concerned about his position as our athletics commentator. There were new names coming up, after all.

He showered and spruced himself up again for his encounter with Cliff, eventually entering the office with, "Frightfully sorry about that little cock-up this morning, Cliffie. I do hope it won't affect my chances of going to Montreal."

"Montreal?" said Morgan. "Montreal? You'll be bloody lucky if you go to the Albert fucking Hall!"

Norman did not go to the Montreal Olympics.

Stories of Cliff went down well in Monmouth, where we also reprised our tales of another great Welsh character in broadcasting, Alun Williams. The two were sometimes at odds, we recalled, leading to one saying of the other – we couldn't remember which way round it went, because it could easily have been uttered by either man – "He came across the room towards me, his eyes ablaze with insincerity."

The only problem with the otherwise delightful Savoy Theatre in Monmouth was technical. The sound system packed up on us halfway through. Fortunately the theatre is small enough that we were able to press on, but at the remote farmhouse bed and breakfast where we were staying, our landlady said, "Yes, I used to go to film shows there, but the sound system kept packing up!"

Sound problems were something we had to deal with from time to time, particularly in our early days. Usually it was just one of our microphones failing, or sometimes, particularly in the case of Blowers, the clip-on lapel microphone he had attached to his shirt slipping down inside it, to treat the audience to the grumblings of his stomach. While such problems were being solved, I tended to tell the old and well-worn Brian Johnston story of the time he asked an audience if they could all hear him. A man in the front row called out, "I can, but I'll willingly change places with someone who can't."

The day after the Monmouth show we were on at the Brighton Theatre Royal, a very different and much grander kettle of fish. For once I included a tale told by Peter O'Toole on *Test Match Special*'s *View from the Boundary* lunchtime spot at the Oval in 1991; as it happened, the day after the infamous 'leg-over' incident (of which, more anon). This was prompted by a discussion on the whole aspect of 'corpsing' on stage, for which O'Toole was notorious.

He admitted to having been twice in stage productions in which the curtain had to be brought down. On that very stage in Brighton he was in a play that he said was not very successful and "not destined for a long life". It was set on a beach and the back of the stage was the sea, represented by plenty of gauzes and lights. His own entrance was from the sea, accompanied by Sylvia Syms; both of them in swimming costumes.

On the beach was an actor called Nicholas Meredith, who had a reputation as "a great giggler". He had to greet O'Toole's character with, "Good morning, Roger", and then erect a deckchair, while delivering his next line, "There's something about a deckchair – austerity, poise and comfort. The austerity is an illusion, the comfort is achieved only with difficulty and the poise we leave to Pamela." Pamela was Sylvia Syms' character.

O'Toole claimed that not once during the run of the play did Meredith manage to get the chair up. When pushed towards an explosion of giggles, Meredith had a habit of twisting his hair into a spike and coughing. On this one occasion the twisting and the coughing had reached epic proportions when, after a long wrestle with the chair, he abandoned it as "a crumpled mass of timber and canvas and, saying, 'I'm going to post a letter,' he marched off into the sea."

It was a situation which had by now reduced O'Toole to hysteria as well, so he took refuge behind a wooden palm tree, while Meredith was floundering around in the gauzes of the 'sea', setting off sparks as he crashed into the electrics. That brought a fireman onto the stage and, faced with the disintegration of the play, the curtain came slowly down. O'Toole assured us that, although everyone seemed to be blaming him as the usual cause of chaos, on this occasion he was totally innocent.

That autumn tour took us on to Bolton, Camberley, Tewkesbury, Liverpool and Grimsby. The latter was on the eve of Blowers' seventy-fourth birthday and he had said that he really was not keen on waking up in Grimsby on such an occasion. So, after the show, we drove to our old favourite hotel, Langar Hall near Nottingham and saw in the first hour of his birthday with whisky and cheese in the drawing room there.

Contrasting theatres in Exeter and Southampton, one reminiscent of a school hall and the other as large as an aircraft hangar, led us to our biggest evening so far – the Cadogan Hall, just off Sloane Street in West London. An enormous stage, more accustomed to hosting orchestras, awaited us in this converted church. The audience, too, was the biggest we'd had so far, many of them known to us, which puts a strange pressure on performance. But it went very well and got a splendid reaction.

Our autumn tour – and our time under Neil O'Brien's management – concluded with shows in Malvern, St Albans, Tunbridge Wells, York and Lowestoft. In the last of those the stage manager informed us that the nearest motorway to the town was in Belgium. After a tortuous journey there, I did not need any convincing.

John Arlott

Brian Johnston (here with PB)

Jonathan Agnew being mischievous in the commentary box.

Christopher Martin-Jenkins struggling with technology.

The development of the set -
Minimalist in Bury St. Edmunds in 2012 (above);
cosy in Norwich in 2014 (below).

Blofeld and Baxter in full flow

Two magnificent old playhouses - Richmond's Georgian theatre (above)
and the Theatre Royal, Bury St. Edmunds (below).

Mr and Mrs Blofeld take coffee - Henry and Valeria in Edinburgh

Valeria at the merchandise stall

Emma Brunjes puts the final touches to the big map -
and it's finally in action on stage in the Spiegeltent.

Off on the bus - we've just done our last show in Oxford.

At the end of a year that had taken us from Margate to Edinburgh and Swansea to Colchester, our next show – remarkably – would be in Australia.

- 8 -

Down Under

AT THE END OF our 2013 autumn tour, we bid farewell to the management of Neil O'Brien, who had launched us, perhaps tentatively, but who could blame him? We had done sixty shows and already our new agent, Emma Brünjes, was coming up with dates for a spring tour. But first we had an overseas adventure to contemplate.

With England's cricketers embarking on an Ashes tour of Australia, we would do shows in some of the Test Match cities. Arranged through the auspices of the Melbourne Comedy Festival, we would perform in Perth, Melbourne and Sydney.

To encourage an Australian audience, rather than just relying on travelling England supporters, we felt we needed an Australian element and I immediately suggested our old friend and colleague Tim Lane. Tim had been a very popular member of the *TMS* team for the World Cup in England in 1999 and the Ashes series in 2001, as well as being a familiar voice for many years on ABC Radio commentaries, where, apart from his cricket coverage, he was also known for calling Australian rules football. He had left ABC when he was offered the chance to cover the football on commercial television. Born and raised in Tasmania, he had long been a resident of the Melbourne suburb of St Kilda.

It did mean that we would have another slightly nerve-racking new element. Blowers and I had developed an easy way between us, where we knew each other's game pretty well, so that any going 'off-piste' did not really matter. With a third person involved, this might be more complicated. Over a dinner at the Weld Club in Perth, where Blowers was staying, we listed the stories we were likely to tell, which prompted Tim to add his own ideas to contribute additions to some of them, as well as his own original offerings.

For instance, he told us of one of his earliest commentaries for a local radio station in Launceston in Tasmania, when he was describing an Australian rules game. There is in that sport a manoeuvre in which the ball is hoofed upfield, which is known as an 'up-country punt'. On this occasion, though, Tim came out with the most unfortunate of spoonerisms. Happily it didn't seem to damage his career overmuch.

That story did prompt us to some other tales of spoonerisms. Blowers had committed his own at Lord's in 1990, when Graham Gooch made 333. When he was out, the crowd of course stood to him, as he walked back to the pavilion where we were situated in those days. Blowers kept his silence to allow the sound of the applause to take over. Then, in his own words, "I decided that something faintly Churchillian was required. I metaphorically put my thumbs in my braces and declared, 'Never, in the history of this great ground, has a cloud crapped like this one.'"

I recalled one of Brian Johnston's spoonerisms of which he was far too proud. There was an old Hampshire batsman called Henry Horton, who had a very angular stance at the crease. As I would say, he might be taking guard in Hampshire, but his bottom was heading for Dorset. Brian tried to describe this by saying that he looked as if he was "sitting on a shooting stick", but as Dr Spooner's great invention took over, it did not quite come out like that. For the next couple of years Johnners would take the tape round with him and play it to anyone who would listen.

Blowers would then cap that with the tale of a golf club where a senior member was landed with the task of making a speech in honour of a not-very-popular outgoing president. He tried to say that he was "a wit and a bit of a shanker", but again, it did not quite emerge as intended.

With Tim talking of his home town of Launceston, I recalled a one-day match that England played there in 1982, when I was covering a tour of Australia for the first time. The travelling journalists were rather crammed into a small wooden press box, in the centre of which was a stack of fairly antiquated radio equipment. Half an hour into the game this crackled into life and a voice came out of it, calling out, "Bruce, Bruce, you there, mate?"

Cricket writers have an inbuilt antipathy towards broadcasters, so, rather testily, I was told, "Baxter, shut that thing up. You're the radio man!"

I peered at this unfamiliar apparatus and eventually found a key to press down and respond, "I'm afraid Bruce doesn't seem to be here."

"Never mind," said the voice, "Give us a score, mate."

So I did that. Twenty minutes later the voice came again. "Bruce, Bruce, you there, mate?"

I was a bit quicker off the mark this time and, in the absence of Bruce, gave him another score. This performance went on at regular intervals throughout the first half of the day's play. Soon I was doing reports for wonderful Radio Launceston and, by the interval, there were even short periods of commentary.

Half an hour into the second session, Bruce turned up. He wandered up to the radio kit and wound a handle to ring his studio.

"That you, Bruce?" demanded the voice.

"Aw, mate, look, sorry, me car went crook," offered Bruce.

"Never mind, mate" (and at this point I should remind you that I was on my first tour Down Under at the age of thirty-five), "some kind old gentleman's been helping us out."

Times like that reminded us how much cricket tourists nowadays miss out on because tours are so concentrated on the international matches. Quite apart from the cricketing side of things and the desperately poor preparation for any overseas Test series that today's scheduling gives, they are missing out on seeing the countries they visit properly. We always used to enjoy games in Australia against 'Country XIs' and remember fondly lunchtime entertainments along the lines of 'Gytas, the frisbee-catching wonder-whippet', or the announcer in a small South Australian town who came out with, "There's going to be a change of bowling at the Piggeries End. It's going to be Stormy Gale. And let's hope he puts the wind up the Poms."

As I recall, I think he did.

The first tour of Australia that Blowers covered was the 1968/9 tour by the West Indies, under the captaincy of Gary Sobers. Their first match was against a Western Australian Country XI in the gold-mining town of Kalgoorlie. A small corps of journalists took the train there to report on the two-day game, among them the celebrated cartoonist Paul Rigby, who had already greeted the tour with a cartoon showing a cricket pavilion with two dressing-room doors, one labelled *SOBERS* and the other *DRUNKS*.

Late on their first evening in Kalgoorlie, after a hearty dinner, Rigby said to his journalistic comrades in arms, "Come on, boys, we're going to visit the drums."

The drums in this instance had no musical application, but were the state-sponsored brothels, established for the pleasure of the miners. They were, Blowers would inform our audience, on Hay Street. I would then be able to thank him, on behalf of the audience, for letting us have the address.

The intention, Blowers insists, was a social, rather than professional, visit, because on previous trips Paul Rigby had made friends with the girls in one particular 'drum'. Thus they were calling out their welcome as the party approached and much jollity followed, though Blowers recalls the madam being a little concerned that someone might be after a freebie, not least because, just as the girls had all acquired splendid French names while on the train trip up from Sydney, Rigby introduced his fellow guests with extravagant titles, culminating with our own 'Lord Henry Fitz-Counterpipe'.

The girls' concern was that a rival establishment had had a birthday party recently for one of their number, with a band playing, and they wanted to do something unique for one of their own in a few days' time. After a moment's thought, Rigby retreated to the corridor and, with a broad pen and remarkable dexterity, created a large orchestra on the wall and leading the splendid mural, unmistakably, was Blowers himself.

(Blowers remains convinced that the painted wall is still there, though I scarcely like to ask how he knows.)

Ten years or so later, Henry had acquired almost cult status in Australia, with appearances on ABC Television interval chats and later commentary on commercial radio stations, to the extent that, soon after the floodlight pylons had been erected at the Sydney Cricket Ground, one of them on the infamous 'Hill' was adorned with a banner, proclaiming it to be *THE BESPECTACLED HENRY BLOFLY STAND*. Our hero visited his fans to take up the offer of a beer and a new banner appeared: *HENRY CAN DRINK MORE THAN KEITH MILLER*. Henry is not sure that the great Miller ever sued over this outrageous calumny.

Our first Australian show was in the Subiaco area of Perth, in the Regal, which, as its name suggests, is an old cinema converted into a theatre. Indeed, the old booking office still bore a sign saying *Adults 2/–, Children 1/–,* and it has been a while since Australia had pounds, shillings and pence. We were performing on the third day of the third Test, on which both Henry and Tim were working, so they came pretty hotfoot to the theatre (and pretty hot, too, as the temperature was in the very high thirties). We had a producer from the Melbourne office, Rebecca Austin, to make life a lot easier in setting up the stage, particularly as, for obvious reasons, I did not have my usual car full of props. I did have a small decanter, though, and had experimented with the right colours of available apple juice to give the impression of whisky.

I could see that Tim was a little anxious about how he was going to fit into what had become a comparatively well-oiled routine between Blowers and me, but he did so splendidly, sensing just the right moments for interjections. It was made slightly more difficult by Blowers having done a number of one-man shows before he left England, so that his honed routine for some of the stories was different. But we reined him in and I think we were all three quite pleased with how it went.

The hotels where England's travelling supporters were staying had all been given plenty of publicity leaflets in advance, so the reasonable audience was probably two-thirds British. It would be interesting to see how it might go down with a more Australian crowd.

Our next show, four days later and less than a week before Christmas, was in the centre of Melbourne in a 170-year-old theatre, the Athenaeum in Collins Street.

There are not too many older buildings than that in Australia. Naturally, it claims to be the oldest theatre in Melbourne and certainly there was an air of some of London's old West End theatres about it, both backstage and front of house. We attracted an audience of around four hundred, with, we thought, a fractional Australian majority.

That left Sydney and the Everest Theatre in the Seymour Centre at the university. This was on the second day of the final Test and a reasonable hike across town from the Sydney Cricket Ground, so we had an 8pm start time. But we had a good – and again, probably majority Australian – audience. By now it was really going well. Tim said he finally felt relaxed about it and it seemed a great pity that we were ending the tour at this point.

One rather provocative audience question at the end was, "Why do the Poms have so many foreigners in their cricket team?"

The other two were clearly searching for an appropriate answer, so I just said, "We're just following the lead given by the Australian rugby team." That seemed to get the right response.

- 9 -

Radio

THE IDEA OF PUTTING the Blofeld and Baxter show on the radio had, as far as I could tell, gone quiet after being suggested in Edinburgh, but obviously behind the scenes, Emma Brünjes and Jonathan Harvey of Hat Trick had been talking through the possibilities. In mid February 2014, we all met for serious discussions on the possibilities and suddenly the thing was becoming reality. I did query whether the unexpurgated version of the story of Raju and the bandits on the road to Jamshedpur would be acceptable to the BBC, and was told that it had been run past them and approved in principle. On the evening it went out, the Radio 4 announcer warned of some 'strong language' to come.

The part of the build-up to that story which would apparently have to be cut involved the overenthusiastic pilot on the flight from Bangalore to Calcutta. It made no sense without doing a cod Indian accent and, in these enlightened times, that would not be well received.

(Though no one was concerned about my attempts at Australian or South African accents in other stories.)

I had drawn up a couple of running orders of tales, making sure the best ones were spread between the two shows, and we even got to the point of agreeing a recording date to meet the two Sunday-evening broadcast slots on Radio 4 in the summer. Next, Emma proposed a dry run at a small fifty-seat theatre above a pub – the Hen & Chickens at Highbury Corner in London. This was a venue which, we learnt, attracted quite a few comedians trying out new material.

In the meantime, in Harrogate, we did our first regular performance under the Emma Brünjes banner and with it a promotional video, which included the two of us talking about the show, added to the audience's thoughts as they came out afterwards. As always, it was very gratifying to hear the enthusiasm of the non-cricket lovers who had been pleasantly surprised that they had enjoyed it.

We had originally been booked to go on from Harrogate to Newcastle, but the theatre had, we gathered, cancelled after an autumn show with Jonathan Agnew and Geoff Boycott had not attracted as big an audience as they had expected. They felt, therefore, that they did not want to risk trying to put on another 'cricket show'. It was annoying that they might think we were doing the same thing, which underlined the importance of that publicity video.

The publicist who had been engaged at the last minute in Edinburgh, Paul Sullivan, pulled off a remarkable coup by getting us an appearance on Alan Titchmarsh's ITV afternoon programme. We shared the guest list with Frank Skinner, Coleen Nolan and Philomena Lee, whose life had just been made into a film starring Judi Dench and Steve Coogan. All that, followed by Blowers and Backers, made for a very mixed show.

I told what I reckoned might appeal to a daytime TV audience, the story of the Queen's cake, while Blowers went for an old favourite Johnners story. In 1976 at Headingley, when security had been tightened after the previous year's assault on the Test pitch by supporters of an East End crook called George Davis, a small dog evaded the stewards and ran onto the outfield. Johnners was in his element.

"We've got an intruder! It's a dachshund and it's running into the middle of the ground. I think it's going to spend a penny! Now it's being chased by umpire Tom Spencer, who's trying to shoo it away with a sweater. It's rather a good bullfight. I'll keep you posted on how it goes, but I just want to tell cricket lovers that this dachshund's a fast bowler. And the reason I know that he's a fast bowler is that he's got four short legs and his balls swing both ways!"

Observing the stunned look on Titchmarsh's face, I wasn't sure that that would make the final edit of the show – but it did!

Towards the end of March we gathered in the old drill hall in Chenies Street, just off Tottenham Court Road, bearing a plaque commemorating 'the Bloomsbury Rifles', who had trained there. It somehow created an image of Virginia Woolf with a musket. Now, though, it was more normally home to RADA productions.

For the first time we included some sound clips. In the first show there was Brian Johnston describing a streaker: "A very – er – obvious streaker." As he headed off the field, Brian inevitably had to offer, "I suppose you could call that a cheeky performance. I don't think he's been sunbathing much. He's a little bit lighter down the – er – backside." Then, to Johnners' consternation and cries of alarm, he "climbed over the boundary boards and they were a little bit higher that he expected". In the second show it was John Arlott's glorious commentary on Ted Dexter batting against Wes Hall at Lord's in 1963. ("There is about Dexter, when he chooses to stand up to fast bowling, an air of command, something near majesty.")

We devoted the first half of the second show to Arlott, starting, after that clip, with Blowers recounting his thirsty reputation. "He lived almost entirely by suction." He recalled that every day's lunch interval involved two bottles of claret and that he was a very much better commentator after lunch.

I then talked of the first World Cup Final in 1975, when John described a six from Clive Lloyd as "the stroke of a man knocking a thistle top off with a walking stick", which I always reckon is as clear a picture of the shot into the Mound Stand at Lord's as could be painted. Also in that West Indies innings, with the ball being dispatched to all parts of St John's Wood, he said, "Dickie Bird having a wonderful time, signalling everything including stop to traffic coming on from behind."

In the four-Test series that followed the World Cup, he had great fun with the Australian fast bowler Dennis

Lillee, who used to wear a huge, loose shirt, the size of a nightshirt, unbuttoned most of the way down, which would billow out as he ran in to bowl, with medallions swinging on his bared chest. The shirt might be voluminous, but the trousers, in the fashion of the day, were drainpipe thin. "Lillee comes in; the shirt big enough for two men. If they could get into the trousers."

On the Friday of the Lord's Test, Arlott was given lunch by his publisher, so that his habitual intake of two bottles of claret was exceeded to become three, or, with the publisher paying, maybe even four. So he arrived back in the commentary box, shall we say – mellow. There he found the then director general of the BBC, Ian Trethowan, paying us a visit. So now he was mellow and showing off. A dangerous combination.

Shortly after he took over at the microphone, he had one of the greatest gifts for any commentator: the first-ever streaker at Lord's. This was a rather tubby merchant seaman called Michael Angelo (not the painter). He ran out from the Tavern Stand away to our right, as we sat in the pavilion commentary box. It was actually Trevor Bailey who was the first to see him. He had heard about the craze of streaking, but could not quite remember the word for it. What he said was, "Ah! A freaker!"

That was the word that Arlott took up. "We've got a freaker. Not very shapely. And it's masculine. And I would think it's seen the last of its cricket for the day." He described him jumping the stumps and then, "Ah, now he's had his load. He's being embraced by a blond policeman and led away in front of at least eight thousand people in the Mound Stand – some of whom, perhaps, have never seen anything quite like this before."

In talking about Brian Johnston in the first show, it was inevitable that we would get on to the infamous 'leg-over' incident. It has passed into folklore, having been played countless times on any excuse and we had talked about it on the show before, without ever playing the clip. We decided, though, not to play the whole two minutes, preferring to give the build-up and what was going on behind the scenes.

It happened in 1991, during the final Test of the summer with England playing the West Indies at the Oval. Curtly Ambrose was bowling to Ian Botham and he sent down a bouncer, which Botham got into position to hook. But he found it was a bit too close to the end of his nose for the shot, so he pulled out of it, but in doing so, lost his balance. He realised that he was likely to step on his stumps, so he tried to vault over them and just brushed a bail off with his thigh. So he was out anyway – hit wicket, bowled Ambrose.

Now, we in the BBC had a new cricket correspondent that year; a young fellow called Jonathan Agnew. (I wonder what happened to him?) Shortly after this incident he went on a social visit to his friends upstairs in the press box. There he ran into the correspondent from the *Sun*, who was lamenting the fact that, as he wrote for a 'family newspaper', he couldn't use the line he had thought of; that Botham "couldn't get his leg over". Aggers obviously stored this away in the back of his mind.

As fate would have it, I had rostered on to do the close-of-play wrap-up that day the combination of the veteran

Brian Johnston with our new cricket correspondent, J. Agnew. They had about ten minutes to go through the events of the day, largely for the benefit of those who had not been with us throughout. When they got to the Botham dismissal, they dealt with it matter-of-factly and were just moving into what would have been safer territory, when Aggers, almost as an afterthought, said, "Yes, he just couldn't quite get his leg over."

Brian gave a sort of little hiccup. He always subsequently claimed that for the next thirty seconds he was more professional than at any other time in his life. Sadly, though, it was only for thirty seconds. I spent that time trying to make sure than no one caught his eye, because he was such an inveterate giggler. He had Bill Frindall on his right, who, I felt, could not have heard the remark, because he was usually another big giggler. He just looked slightly bemused as I made him lean back in his chair. On Johnners' left, Aggers was already leaning back, with his shoulders heaving in mirth at his own jest.

Between them, Brian was struggling on manfully, elbows on the desk, head in hands, staring straight ahead. I just about had time to think, *We're going to get away with this.* Then I heard him say, quite quietly at first, "Do stop it, Aggers." At that point I knew we were completely sunk. Sure enough, after a few more seconds, the tears started to roll down his cheeks and a large spotted handkerchief appeared to mop them up.

And at that point of the story we played the soundtrack of the first wheeze from Brian and the strangled, high-pitched, "Oh, Aggers, do stop it!" They both tried to keep the account of the cricket going, but it was a forlorn hope for the next minute or so, until Brian was able to announce, "I've stopped laughing now."

Having said at the outset of our onstage partnership that we would not be using that clip, partly because everyone else did, it seemed likely that we would include it in future. It was irresistible.

It often led, though, to enquiries about why we did not also use the other gaffe for which Johnners was famous: "The bowler's Holding, the batsman's Willey." That was because he never said it. He might have done, with Michael Holding bowling to Peter Willey, though it would not have been his commentary style. I was actually asked to look for the tape for possible use at Brian's memorial service, though what the Dean and Chapter of Westminster Abbey would have made of it, I cannot imagine.

I knew that it did not exist. If he had said it, he would have collapsed into giggles and certainly Bill Frindall would not have missed another one. But my main reason for being certain that it was apocryphal was that the only way we ever heard of it was a single postcard, which said, *You really must be more careful with young people listening. Do you know what you said? "The bowler's Holding, the batsman's Willey."* But it was the signature on the card which clinched it for us. It was signed by a Miss Tess Tickle.

We included in the radio shows another old favourite story of mine, which I had been using in after-dinner speeches for years. On my first tour of India in 1981, the first time I ever produced *TMS* abroad was in Ahmadabad for the first One Day International of that tortuous tour.

There our commentary box was a sort of concrete cave at the back of the stand. That was not ideal, but then a large sheet of scratched Perspex was put across the cave opening to make it difficult to see out, or get any air in, or, it seemed, to establish any communication with the outside world.

The game started and we still had made no contact with London. I was sitting at the commentary desk, with headphones clamped to my ears, calling out, "Hello, London. Hello, Bombay. Hello, anyone beyond the walls of Ahmadabad!"

For half an hour there was no response. Then, far away in the distance, I could hear a faint Indian voice. "Hello, hello."

I was really excited. "Hello, Bombay!" I cried. It must surely be Bombay, through which centre the line to London would be routed.

But the faint voice just went on. "Hello, hello."

I tried again. "Come on, Bombay, we should have been on the air half an hour ago."

Still the faint voice ignored me. "Hello, hello."

Then Tony Lewis, former Glamorgan and England captain, who was one of our commentary team that day, tapped me on the shoulder and indicated a Sikh engineer, headphones stretched over his turban, who was sitting immediately behind me, saying for the umpteenth time, "Hello, hello."

It took quite a bit longer before we raised London to commentate on the last match that England won before they left India almost three months later.

And talk of tours of India brought us Blowers' fine account of his journey there for the 1977/8 England tour, which he undertook with four companions, one of them John Woodcock of the *Times*, in a 1921 Rolls-Royce Silver Ghost, known to its owner as "the old gal", backed up by a new Rover. The cars, insisted Henry, "were by far the least temperamental members of the party". They were sponsored by, amongst others, Long John Scotch whisky, which enabled me to suggest that they were "as sponsored as newts". Their remarkable route, through Europe, Turkey, Iran, Afghanistan and Pakistan, would not long afterwards have been impossible and, incredibly, they arrived at Baroda, about a day's drive out from their destination of Bombay, pretty much on schedule.

There they stayed with their old friend, the Maharaja of Baroda, where, by prior arrangement, Blowers was to sing for his supper by addressing the Baroda Cricket Association in the great hall of the Maharaja's palace. The Baroda Cricket Association, he reckoned, numbered about 2,500 souls and they pretty much filled the hall, with standing room only. Blowers, after being given a rapturous reception, spoke to them for sixty-five minutes and, by his own modest account, "I was absolutely brilliant." They all seemed to lap it up, applauding appropriately and giving him a ten-minute standing ovation at the end.

Then, also in his words, "they all buggered off" and the host and his visitors repaired to the dining hall for dinner. The conversation was lively, but, as often happens, there came a moment when there was a lull and, in the silence, John Woodcock asked the Maharaja, "Prince, how many of that audience would have understood every word of Blowers' speech?"

The Prince had a think. "Practically no one," he said.

- 10 -

Under New Management

IN 2014 WE DID, in all, eighty shows, taking the stage every month from January in Sydney to the end of October in Burnley. In early June in Chipping Norton, we reached the hundredth performance in the two years we'd been doing it.

That hundredth show was a sell-out and the theatre told us they'd even sold half a dozen 'standing only' tickets. Chipping Norton has an unusually high stage. In setting it up, I realised that we would have to be sitting in our armchairs fairly far towards the front edge so that the first two rows could see us at all. In front of the chairs we always had a small, low table with the decanter and a copy of *Wisden* on it as props. The main purpose of the *Wisden* was to conceal the clock we needed to give us an idea of how we were going.

As we started the second half of the show, I realised the clock had disappeared. In fact the whole table had disappeared, though I eventually located it in a far corner of the stage. I said, "Blowers, we seem to have lost our table."

From the darkness of the auditorium came a voice. "Yes, I moved it because I couldn't see you."

So, when we were coming up to the question session at the end, I told the audience, "If you've got buses to catch, just go, because we've lost our clock and so we've got no idea of how long we've done!" But I don't think the good folk of Chipping Norton often catch buses, because there was no stampede.

Some venues stick very happily in the memory, like the Tivoli Theatre in Wimborne, not least because it was another enthusiastic full house. We stayed with a friend of Blowers' who lived opposite the theatre and we borrowed armchairs from a friend of hers who lived next door. All delightfully local! It produced an isolated couple of cheers from the audience when we came on stage and I stopped and said, "What very nice furniture, Blowers!"

The Little Theatre in Chorley was another cosy experience, not least because the Mayor invited us to tea in his parlour before the show. Both that theatre and the one in Wimborne are run by volunteers. That can be a bit of a tyranny, but in those cases it works very well.

By contrast to that cosiness, there was the Colosseum in Watford, which, we were told, holds two thousand. It certainly looked as if the airship R101 could have been parked in it and still have left room for the *Hindenburg* alongside it. They proudly told us that all the great orchestras loved to perform there on account of its wonderful acoustic. That did not make it any less daunting for two old blokes in armchairs, though. We had a decent enough audience, perhaps in excess of three hundred, but they were lost in that space and, while we were assured later that they had enjoyed it, none of that reaction reached us on stage.

At the interval, as we walked off through the wings, I said to Blowers, "God, that was hard work."

Overhearing this, the stage manager offered, "Yes, all the comedians die here."

In May we headed north to Aberdeen, by way of a show in Berwick-upon-Tweed at the Maltings. Shortly before this, Blowers told me that we had been invited to stay for a couple of nights either side of our appearance at the Lemon Tree in Aberdeen by one of his fellow old Etonians. "A chap called Forbes," he said. This turned out to be Lord Forbes, head of the clan Forbes, who entertained us royally at Castle Forbes.

Aberdeen's Lemon Tree did us well with another full house. Though, as we were setting up in the afternoon, a problem did start to present itself. There was another auditorium on the site and an American heavy metal band were performing there that night. The sound of their rehearsal made it clear that we simply could not be on at the same time as them. So negotiations were entered into. They agreed to a slightly delayed start and we agreed to shorten our interval and, by the skin of our teeth, we avoided overlapping, though it was hard to have any conversation during our post-show book signing.

One other unfortunate piece of scheduling hit us when we appeared at the Lowther Pavilion in Lytham. England's match against Uruguay kicked off in the World Cup football in Brazil at just about the same time as we took the stage. There was an unusually high female majority in the audience and their menfolk might just have saved themselves a bit of pain if they'd come along to see us, because Uruguay won 2–1.

Lytham, on the Lancashire coast, was the second day in a testing four-day trek. We'd been in Sheffield the night before, and the night after were in Hunstanton on the Norfolk coast, followed by a full Saturday-night house at the Kenton Theatre in Henley. In Hunstanton, the theatre was called the Princess, apparently renamed in honour of Diana, Princess of Wales. We were told that she used to bring the young Princes William and Harry there. The Sandringham Estate is very close. The enterprising stage manager had secured the loan of a couple of suitable armchairs from an hotel about two hundred yards away across the green. She and I carried them over to the theatre, to the amusement of holidaymakers enjoying the afternoon sunshine.

We had become very wary of shows in university campus theatres. The name of the theatre did not always give the game away until we got there. Thus the Strode in Street in Somerset and the Hawthorne in Welwyn Garden City on this run of shows came as unwelcome surprises. It is not that there is necessarily anything wrong with the theatres, in fact most of them have great facilities, but there seems habitually to be a complete lack of any proper publicity. While we might attract a few enthusiasts from the student population, our audience was more likely to come from outside and, to be frank, to be from an older generation. In a university theatre a poster might be put up in the foyer, but that would probably be the extent of it. And later you might hear the old familiar, "Oh, I wish we'd known you were doing that."

In our early days we had had the double whammy of a campus theatre and a Sunday evening, when we played the Gulbenkian in Canterbury – in every other respect a delightful theatre. On this tour we returned to Canterbury for an appearance at the Marlowe. Two theatres are side by side in the same building there and that night the larger auditorium was starring Derren Brown, the mind reader. The management had staggered start times a little, so that the audiences did not get too mixed up, which worked until the interval, which came at just about the same time for each of us, causing, I gathered later, chaos at the bar.

There was one other problem, in that Derren Brown's show used radio microphones to hear from members of the audience. We also used radio mics ourselves on stage and apparently all the systems went through the control room of the larger theatre. That would not necessarily have been a problem, except that the Brown show did not need them after halfway through each act, at which point they switched the system off. That meant that Blowers and I found ourselves having to project a bit more to reach the back of a fair-sized and pretty well-filled theatre from midway through each half.

We had changed agents to come under Emma Brünjes' wing largely on the back of her expertise on the Edinburgh Fringe, so in 2014 we were again heading for the Scottish capital for August, this time to do almost the full month.

Over a weekend stay at Emma's splendid family home in Sussex, we tried out our one-hour Fringe show, having to make a few cuts of favourite stories to fit it into the time.

We arrived in Edinburgh at the end of July to find fliers that announced we were *Returning by popular demand!* How true that might be, I was not sure, but it was nice to read. This time we were nearer the centre of the university buildings, in the Pleasance Dome, which had the considerable advantage, in a fairly wet August, of having a large covered area serving several theatres, while providing food and drink stalls.

Our auditorium featured a horseshoe arrangement of staged seating, which had apparently originally been built for a Tony Blair lecture tour, so that it could be dismantled and stored for the other eleven months of the year. Its tight curve meant that one evening, as Blowers was telling our audience about Brian Johnston, I found myself looking past his shoulder straight into the eyes of Ian Johnston, Brian's youngest son. I debated whether to inform Henry of this on stage, but decided it might throw him off track.

Our American stage manager was not a great fan of ours, but the reviewers were kind – even the *Daily Telegraph*, with a back-page article, and the *Times*, who gave us a four-star review, unfortunately only three days before the end of our run, though they did plug our autumn tour.

As a bit of a publicity exercise, Emma had planned a cricket match to be played on the Meadows – 'Talent v Industry'. The unquestionably talented Joe Stilgoe, inheriting his father's love of the game, was to captain the former team, and the producer, Steve Marmion, the latter. We did a reconnaissance visit to the proposed ground; to my surprise, one of several cricket pitches on the Meadows. All seemed set, but the weather had other ideas and we had to cancel, in the face of wind, driving rain and a forecast of worse to come.

Talk in Edinburgh was inevitably about the impending referendum on Scottish independence, so that, as I left, I wondered if we would be returning next year to a separate country. With a good deal of Scottish blood in my veins (but, of course, like so many Scots living over the border, no vote), I sincerely hoped not. As it happened, referendum day saw us doing a show at the Opera House in Buxton and we sat up in front of the TV that night in our B&B, anxiously watching the first results coming in. Fortunately, common sense prevailed.

Four days later we were on the West End stage at the Lyric Theatre in front of a large audience, many of whom were known to us – just to add to the tension – not least one drama professor, my own ninety-nine-year-old aunt. But fortunately, it was a triumph. The theatre was having a night off from its current run of *Thriller*, which explained the Michael Jackson wig on a stand in the dressing room I was using.

I suppose, after that, it was inevitable that we should be brought back to earth, and two nights later we were at the Civic Theatre in Rotherham. It was a perfectly good theatre and a receptive audience, but the show was punctuated by a loud voice from the front row. "Tell us about Geoffrey Boycott. We want to hear about Boycott!" The owner of the voice came up to us as we signed books afterwards. "Quite good," he said, "but you should have more about Geoffrey Boycott!"

In fact, whenever the question session threw up a request for a story about Geoffrey, I would offer an incident from South Africa in 1995. The *TMS* commentary was a joint operation with the South African Broadcasting Corporation. They mounted a commentary in Afrikaans, while we did the English-language commentary for ourselves and, for half the time, for them. They would switch between the two in half-hour spells. There was also a period in the day when we had to negotiate *The Daily Service* and *Yesterday in Parliament* on Radio 4 long wave.

So there were sometimes spells when we were not actually live on the air for anyone. SABC were away for a half-hour of Afrikaans, while the UK audience were hearing of the goings-on at Westminster. During these times we would do a relaxed sort of commentary to record any highlights we might need later. Jonathan Agnew, being pretty savvy about such matters, spotted such a fifteen-minute slot coming up during the latter stages of the Johannesburg Test. Before he started doing the sort of commentary necessary for the recording, he checked with me that we really were going out nowhere live.

After a few minutes he was joined by Geoff Boycott, who was obviously, as he settled into the summariser's chair, unaware that we were not on the air. Aggers carried on commentating on what was turning out to be a remarkable rear-guard (and ultimately match-saving) innings by Mike Atherton. After describing another defensive shot he offered, "Well, you'd know about this sort of thing, Geoffrey. You were a pretty boring batsman."

Geoffrey looked a little startled as Aggers described the next block. "Yes," he went on, "you used to send the crowd to sleep. In fact, they always say that Botham used to empty the bars; you used to fill them."

Boycott tried to find something to say, without a lot of success. Aggers persisted with this line between each ball, finishing with, "God, you were boring!" and then, "Welcome back, Radio 4 listeners, to *Test Match Special*. We haven't been on the air to anyone for the last quarter of an hour, but Geoffrey Boycott thought we were."

A bemused Boycott could only smile sheepishly and admit that he'd been done by a master.

One of our new stories concerned another celebrity, though. Blowers had taken Valeria out for lunch in London, where he was aware of some pretty young women at another table enjoying a lively meal with an older man. After a bit, the man came over to speak to him, apologising for disturbing his lunch. He asked him to sign a menu. "Just to Mick," he said.

Blowers, a little grumpy to have a fan interrupting the meal, signed and looked up into the face of Sir Mick Jagger.

Our usual set of stories about Brian Johnston now included mention of his splendid ears and the trick he had of folding them into themselves. He was liable to do this in the commentary box, then catch the eye of whoever was commentating, before completing the trick by raising an eyebrow so that the folded ear popped out again to resume its previous glory.

That inevitably led us on to recall another even more splendid pair of ears, which belonged to an old Australian friend of ours, Bernie Leverington. Some sort of valuable mineral had been discovered on his land in South Australia, which had made him rich enough to travel the world with his wife, Kay, watching Test cricket. They often stayed at the same hotels as the *TMS* team, so we got to know them pretty well.

On one occasion we were all at Brockencote Hall, in the Worcestershire village of Chaddesley Corbett, for an Edgbaston Test. Blowers had finished his last commentary spell for the day some time before the close of play, so had slipped away to avoid the rush. That meant that he was at least a bottle ahead of us when we returned and, during the dinner that followed, it was a lead he was able to maintain.

In another section of the dining room, Kay and Bernie Leverington finished their meal and their route out wound between tables to come right past the one where about eight of us were eating. Kay was leading – a fine, Junoesque figure of a woman, with an extensive décolletage. Blowers, well-brought-up chap that he is, got, admittedly rather unsteadily, to his feet. He swayed slightly, backwards and forwards. It was on the forward sway, with ample cleavage confronting him, that he uttered his greeting. To the astonishment of all of us it was, "Hello, Boob!"

Fortunately, Bernie, despite the impressive ears, was fairly deaf.

There was one other Johnners line which I would sometimes throw in, remembering when CMJ had introduced him to the microphone with, "After a word from Trevor Bailey, it will be the old master."

As Johnners sat down, he was saying, "Did he call me an old bastard?"

We finished our year with an intense flourish, including one run of six shows in seven days from Cranleigh in Surrey to Whitley Bay in Northumberland. Amongst that was a bit of a homecoming for Blowers when we went to the Maddermarket in Norwich. He was able to stay with his brother on the estate at Hoveton where he grew up. As we set off from there into the city in the afternoon, he announced authoritatively, "Follow me. I know Norwich well!"

I was able to tell a packed audience that evening, "So do I now. We went round it about five times before we found the theatre."

My own homecoming was a few days later at the Stables in Wavendon, on the outskirts of Milton Keynes, so within a quarter of an hour's drive for me. It was a theatre I had been keen for us to do, and not just for that helpful geographical fact. It is a delight, as was having the then England cricket captain, Alastair Cook, in the audience. He was polite enough to say he enjoyed it!

We ended that autumn tour with the prospect of eight shows coming up in New Zealand in February, for which the dates and venues were pretty well finalised, and then on to Kuala Lumpur, Singapore, Hong Kong and Colombo in March. Detailed plans for travel were being laid, not least with Cathay Pacific giving us a free flight out and back for the use of our two radio shows on their entertainment system. Exciting times! Though, as we went into winter, it all did seem to go a little ominously quiet on the planning front. That never bodes well.

- 11 -

Rogues on the Road

EARLY IN 2015 IT became apparent that both our local agents on the ground who were laying plans for our shows in New Zealand and South-East Asia had let us down. That tour would not be happening, which was a big disappointment.

However, Emma Brünjes was already looking ahead to the Edinburgh Festival. She decided that it must be a completely new show. No more reposing in the armchairs. There must be movement! Blowers and I looked at each other not quite with panic, but perhaps mild concern. She had also, the previous autumn, decided that we ought to do a full professional photo shoot, so we had a day of outfit changes, surrounded by various props, mostly suggesting travel.

What Emma had proposed was a show based on overseas touring. And to support it, she had the idea of the backdrop of a large map of the world on which we could pin flags – or perhaps luggage labels – as we told a story related to each place. A new show title was also needed to replace our original *Memories of Test Match Special*. It was Blowers who came up with *Rogues on the Road*.

We discussed a different opening. Emma was all for changing the music, though Henry and I both spoke up for the *TMS* theme, 'Soul Limbo', given the precious audience reaction to those opening beats. I thought maybe some appropriate commentary clips could be laid over it, and then came the suggestion of it being interrupted by the 'bing-bong' of an airport announcement calling us for a flight.

But our biggest problem was recalling enough previously untold anecdotes to fill first a one-hour Edinburgh show and then two hours on an autumn tour. We had, after all, used what we reckoned was our best material over the last three years. A number of brainstorming sessions were called for, in which we just listed every sort of touring story we could think of.

Meanwhile, Emma commissioned a designer to make the map. The first draft I saw was a bit too impressionistic, giving the world a rather distorted look. It had, after all, to be slightly usable as a map if we were going to be able to pinpoint the places we were talking about. So the designer went – quite literally – back to the drawing board. It was unlikely to be ready much before we got to Edinburgh, so some sort of substitute had to be sorted out for us to rehearse with in the warm-up shows. I pinned a large map to a cork board and tied labels to coloured pins. I thought the best way of labelling them was to use the international three-letter code for each airport – LHR for Heathrow, for instance, BNE for Brisbane, CCU for Calcutta, etc. Whether the audience would be able to see this stand-in map properly, from further back than the front row at any rate, was doubtful. And they would not be able to read the lettering on the labels, but the main purpose at the moment was for us to see how it would work.

Emma had also suggested a waist-high table, known, I soon discovered, as a 'poseur table', which seemed appropriate for a couple of poseurs to stand by. Separate from that, she suggested a couple of high stools. I reckoned that everything needed to be folding, so that I could transport the set in my car, with the advantage that we would no longer have to depend on the theatres finding appropriate armchairs. The stools I found in a quaint little boutique called IKEA, and the table online.

We needed to try out our new material, so again a pub theatre was booked, this time at the Tabard in Chiswick in June, where our usual rule about Sunday evenings being bad news did not seem to apply and we got a near-full house. (Cheap tickets, I think!)

Our new introduction was used in anger for the first time. It consisted of a mix with the usual start of 'Soul Limbo' and the two commentary clips, which I had honed down to a little under twenty seconds each, laid over the music. First Blowers' commentary on the end of the 1987 World Cup final in Calcutta ("Now you really can charge those glasses in Australia. I give you my final, final permission…"), followed by my own commentary on the end of the 1992 final in Melbourne, when Pakistan beat England. Then came the 'bing-bong' and, with a splendid airport tannoy effect, Emma Brünjes' voice: "This is an urgent and final call for passengers Blofeld and Baxter. That's passengers Blofeld and Baxter for Flight BA 589 to Calcutta. The gates close in five minutes. Would Blofeld and Baxter leave the bar immediately and proceed to Gate 5, which is about to close."

After the first few shows and before we went to Edinburgh, we realised that the laugh came on 'leave the bar immediately', so with a nifty bit of editing, it was tightened up, so we could make a rushed entrance on that note. Again, after a few try-outs, we gave Blowers a glass to be carrying and put down at the edge of the stage, as if he really had been hurried out of the bar.

There was a slightly different introduction for the second act. It was 'Soul Limbo' again, but now I had put together a montage of commentary clips of Blowers describing non-cricketing things round the ground.

An airport-related story was required to start us off and Blowers had one. This concerned a tour of Australia when he had stayed on for a few days in Sydney, because he had met a gorgeous blonde and was enjoying her company to the full. Sometime after he returned home, late one evening, he was thinking of this beauty and, on an impulse, picked up the phone and rang her.

"I don't suppose you'd like to come to Paris for the weekend?" he asked. She did indeed like the idea and agreed to meet him in London in a few days' time.

So, a very excited Henry went to Heathrow, inevitably far too early for the flight, watching the emerging passengers anxiously. They came through in their droves, but there was no familiar tall, willowy blonde. Eventually, though, his eye did light on a rather dumpy brunette who seemed vaguely familiar. "Hello," he said, unable to remember her name, "my dear old thing, what brings you here?"

"Don't you remember?" she replied. "You invited me to come to Paris for the weekend!"

It seemed he had dialled the wrong number.

After a momentary hesitation, as the penny dropped, he grabbed her bags, not so much out of gallantry, but just so that he could have a look at the labels and ascertain her name.

At this point in the disgraceful narrative, I could interrupt on behalf of the audience, to ask, "So did you take her to Paris?"

She had indeed gone with him for what turned out to be a less-than-perfect weekend.

That version of the story stayed until November, when we found ourselves doing a show the day after the terrorist attack on the Bataclan Theatre in Paris. That evening I suggested that somehow it seemed inappropriate to talk with such levity about a trip to that city. So it became Monte Carlo, which subsequently I felt Blowers thought had a bit more élan about it and so the story stayed with that location. Indeed, when he appeared as a panellist on the television show *Would I Lie to You?*, he told that tale and the opposition guessed wrongly that it was a lie.

I had an airport story to add from – inevitably – India. Early in 2002 England were there for a fairly intense one-day series, with a match every three days, and travel and practice days in between. After one game in Cuttack, Jonathan Agnew and I were booked next morning on a flight from Bhubaneswar, where we were staying, to Madras, soon to change its name to Chennai in order to confuse travellers. We arrived at the airport check-in desk in good time. The man behind it looked a little confused and then had to admit, "Your flight is delayed."

"For how long?"

"For just seven hours." He looked a little gloomy, but then suddenly brightened up. "But you are entitled to free meal!" And he backed up this offer of largesse by opening a drawer and producing an unwrapped sandwich on a plate.

We decided that maybe we did have time to go back to the hotel for our lunch after all.

"Never mind," he said and put the sandwich back in the drawer, no doubt to await the next hungry would-be passenger.

We used that story a couple of times, but then my wife, Kim, suggested the inclusion instead of a favourite of hers. It was an incident from an already fairly eventful tour of India in 1984, when David Gower was England's captain. The last match before the first Test was played in Rajkot, about three hundred miles to the north-west of Bombay. There was a daily return flight there from Bombay which happened as regularly as clockwork – or at least as nearly clockwork-like as any transport in India did in those days.

On the day in question the England cricket team were on board, with the accompanying press, flying down to Bombay for the start of a Test series which had been delayed by the assassination of Mrs Gandhi. As we approached our destination, the pilot invited Gower up to the cockpit for the landing, something which was not so unusual then, though it would not be allowed now. In the cabin, we passengers were aware of our losing height and flying over Bombay, before turning over the Western Ghats, the escarpment to the east of the city. We flew over Bombay again, turned over the Arabian Sea and repeated our journey back to another turn over the Western Ghats.

We must have made at least half a dozen passes over Bombay before we eventually landed. As we came to rest outside the terminal building, Gower emerged from the flight deck, laughing. We were keen to find out what had been going on.

"Well," he said, "it went something like this." And he proceeded to tell us the tale.

As we had approached and the pilot began his descent, he had contacted air traffic control. "Bombay Tower, this is Flight 201 from Rajkot. Request permission to land."

There was a stunned silence from the air traffic controller. Then, "Who are you? You are not on my list! Go away, please."

The pilot tried again. "Bombay Tower, this is Flight 201 – *daily* flight from Rajkot. Request permission to land."

There was a long sigh from the air traffic controller. "You silly fellow! I have told you already, you are not on my list. Now, go away, please."

So we flew on, out over the Ghats and back over the Arabian Sea a few more times, before the pilot decided that he had one more card up his sleeve. "Bombay Tower, I am running out of fuel."

There was another exasperated sigh from the controller. "Oh, all right, then," he conceded. "But don't make a habit of it!"

So we landed – and lost the Test Match.

Blowers had another crisis in the air to relate. Early in 1981 he had been reporting on an England tour of the Caribbean, for which Ian Botham was captain. It was a tour beset by a number of troubles and one of those, Blowers wrote in the *Sunday Express*, was Botham's captaincy. It consisted, according to Henry, of *waving his arms around like a great big baby*.

The *Sunday Express* inevitably highlighted this and someone cut the article out and sent it to Botham. He stuck it in a blazer pocket to be read at a later date, but had no occasion to wear that blazer before the flight home. That flight came about forty-eight hours after the end of the final Test in Jamaica, and in those forty-eight hours the team and its accompanying press made serious inroads into Jamaica's rum stocks. So some of the legs eventually ascending the steps onto the London flight were none too steady.

On the plane, Blowers was stationed a few rows behind the England captain who, according to him, was "sitting between two of the great Yorkshire intellectuals. And, no, I have to tell you, Geoffrey Boycott was not one of them. They were Graham Stevenson and dear old Bluey – David – Bairstow. Delving in his blazer pocket, Botham found the newspaper clipping and read it. The brains trust he was with agreed with him that Blofeld should be sorted out when the plane landed in Bermuda."

To everyone's surprise, when they did land in Bermuda, Bernard Thomas, the long-serving physiotherapist, organised a session of physical jerks for the team. This was not so much for their fitness as to keep I. T. Botham away from H. C. Blofeld. However, when the session ended, Botham went in pursuit of his quarry and found him in the bar. There he demanded that Henry accompany him outside. Blowers found that he was happier to stay where he was. However, he was lifted by the lapels – as one witness described it, "as if he was going to hang him on the coat hooks on the wall". When dropped, Henry felt it safer to remain on the floor, where the efficiency of any further assault proved to be impaired by his assailant's earlier intake of rum.

Back on the plane for the onward flight to London, Blowers found that he had another piece of good fortune. While for the first leg from Kingston he had had an empty seat next to him, it was now occupied by a beautiful, curvaceous blonde. He looked forward to her company for the flight.

Shortly after take-off from Bermuda, though, his first overtures were interrupted by the arrival of the England captain advancing down the aisle, still enraged, with fist raised. Blowers could see trouble ahead and thought it wise to remove his glasses and pass them for safekeeping to his lovely neighbour. He slipped them under his arm and encountered soft resistance. He pushed a little harder and the resistance became firmer, until the lady leapt into the air with a loud, "How dare you?!" And he discovered that he had been pushing his spectacles into her ample left boob.

Now he had hostility on both sides, but rescue came in the form of a steward who persuaded Botham to return to his seat, leaving our hero to make amends to his fair companion. By the time they landed, he had coaxed a phone number out of her, but the next day he discovered that it had been a false one.

The press party agreed not to write about the incident, but somehow the story was leaked and made the front page of the following Sunday's *People*.

Sometimes you try to use a story that just does not work. The tale of *TMS* being locked out of a ground in Sri Lanka is often used by people introducing me for an after-dinner speech, but, though it is a reasonable account of the potential trials of touring, its main problem for use on stage is that it has no punchline.

It happened in 2001. An under-the-table deal had been done by the Sri Lankan Cricket Board with talkSPORT radio for the commentary rights and the BBC had not been allowed to bid. It meant that we were restricted to reporting no more than two minutes in every hour during play. However, the board at some stage realised that they had missed a chance for more revenue by not having a bidding process and now felt that they should be charging rights for reporting. So, on the second morning of the first Test in Galle, we found ourselves barred from the ground. The thing that caught media attention was that I sent

Jonathan Agnew round to the ramparts of the old Dutch fort that overlooks the ground, with a decent view of the scoreboard, to send his reports via satellite phone. I stayed outside the gates to try to negotiate with the board.

It was all sorted out by lunchtime, with the good offices of the England and Wales Cricket Board's chief executive, Tim Lamb. When invited to recount the story in the onstage question sessions, the only way I could get a reasonable finish was to tell of having Aggers' perch on the walls pointed out to me from the committee box while I accepted a third gin and tonic. We left the story out of our running order.

Blowers had a tale, which we only used a couple of times, of dictating a piece to his newspaper from Australia before going out on the town. When he returned, in a fairly well-oiled mood, he saw the copy lying on the desk and couldn't remember sending it, so he rang up and dictated it to the copytaker in London. Waking up in the morning with a bit of a hangover, he saw the piece still sitting there and still had no recollection of transmitting it, so he called up the copytaker.

After a bit he checked with the sports editor that they'd got the piece. "Was it all right?" he asked.

"Oh yes," came the reply, "but I'm not sure it was quite good enough to merit being sent three times."

After the Tabard, we had our first opportunity to try out the one-hour version of the show on a Sunday afternoon at the City of London Festival. Unfortunately, while we would have liked to have been concentrating on developing the show, we ended up battling the problems of the venue, which was a lower-ground-floor conference room in an hotel near St Paul's. We arrived to find a very grumpy sound man, who had only been told that we needed to play music and clips at the last minute. The overhead lighting was down one side of the room – unfortunately the opposite side from the one where our very small dais had been placed. The dais was too small for both our table and our tall chairs, and our map had to be propped up on a pedestal just off the stage.

There had been some confusion over the venue beforehand and it was barely signposted on the day, so the eighty people who managed to make up our audience did well to find us. But we got through it, and days like that are all part of show business, I suppose.

Our appearance at the Holt Festival in Norfolk a few weeks later was presented with slightly different problems. We were in an open-air theatre in the woods at Gresham's School. They had given us a splendidly furnished dressing room in a tent in the woods behind the stage, with a selection of cricket memorabilia thoughtfully intended to make us feel at home. For a change, we had been told that what was required was an hour-and-a-quarter's show.

Our main problem was that we were on in the late afternoon and the evening's show was Steve Harley & Cockney Rebel. Obviously, they were much more concerned with getting the stage set up and doing the sound checks for the band than for us, and I had to put my foot down, as the audience were about to start wending their way through the trees, to demand our own quick check on sound clips and setting up on the narrow front-of-stage strip that had been left for us.

A couple of run-throughs for Emma's benefit and we were ready to take the road to Edinburgh and the first reveal of the great map!

- 12 -

The Spiegeltent

AUGUST 12TH IS KNOWN in field sports circles as the 'Glorious Twelfth'. For Blowers and me in 2015 it was surely glorious for the opening of *Rogues on the Road* at the Edinburgh Fringe. First thing that morning we had our initial sight of the big map which was to be our working backdrop. And it was big – three metres square, we were told, which I translated into English as being about ten feet.

Our stage for this, our third appearance at the Fringe, was in George Square, in the Spiegeltent. This circular structure, almost like a circus big top, with fixed tables round the walls and a dance floor in the centre, had its origin a century ago in Belgium. There was a stage at one side with a bar opposite and the tent was capable, we heard, of holding an audience of four hundred. It was certainly our grandest Edinburgh venue so far, though we did encounter a bit of a problem as the roof of the tent rose to a peak over the dance floor, which was the centre of the auditorium for us. The roof then, like any tent, sloped down to its walls, which meant that over our stage there was not quite as much as the ten-feet clearance we needed to hang our map.

Fortunately, in true Fringe tradition, we had a very resourceful stage crew who constructed a support frame for the map on scaffold poles. We also had the benefit of the best backstage area we had yet enjoyed at the Fringe after two years of hiding behind a curtain at the side of the stage (it could scarcely be described as 'in the wings'). We could now wait in comfort, even with a cup of coffee and, glory be, a loo!

Emma Brünjes had asked me to list the places round the world which would feature in our tales and had then painstakingly sewed Velcro spots onto the map at the appropriate places herself – a very hard job, as I was to discover over the next couple of years whenever we needed to add a new destination. The map material was thick and the Velcro spots similarly resistant to a needle. I had checked the airport codes for the relevant places and the designer had made outsize luggage labels to be attached to the various spots. An interesting geography test!

One of the airport codes I had checked – just for an ironic variation – was Nottingham (NQT, if you're interested), so that Blowers could tell one of his oldest favourite stories, which had rather dropped out of his recent repertoire.

It happened in the earlier stages of his journalistic career. He had just been reporting on a county championship match in the north of England and his next assignment was Nottinghamshire v Gloucestershire at Trent Bridge. At the end of the first day's play he had a drink with a couple of the Gloucestershire players and then went to check into his hotel.

Blowers is a fan of smaller hotels with a bit of character about them, but in those days his office would place a higher imperative on the cost and would use various chains of modern, functional establishments. The layout of the rooms always seemed to be identical.

He left his bags in another such poky room and headed to the restaurant for a solitary dinner, washed down – abstemiously – with a bottle and a half of red wine, though he normally deplores half-bottles as "keyhole surgery". So he repaired to bed, feeling "very nicely, thank you".

Now, Blowers is not a fan of wearing pyjamas in bed – and I realise that this information should have come with a prior health warning. From his teens he has always slept in a natural state. He went straight to sleep, but was woken by an insistent call of nature. Knowing the layout of all these modern hotel rooms, he had no need to put the light on and made his way to the bathroom door. He was slightly surprised to find a bright light on and then to find a blank wall three feet in front of him. As the significance of this was sinking in, he heard a clunk behind him of a heavy room door closing.

The penny dropped. He was stark naked in the tenth-floor corridor of the hotel. He assessed the crisis: "My parents spent a great deal on my education," he said, "but no one ever prepared me for a situation like this."

He obviously needed to find the night porter, so he looked around for stairs or a fire escape, without success.

He would have to risk the lift. Making his way in that direction, he found a used tea tray outside one of the room doors. Under the cup and saucer was a paper doily. It seemed to be the only available protection for his modesty, so he picked it up and, in his words, "it just about did the trick".

When we introduced this story, I got hold of a packet of doilies and would leave one on the table for him to use as a demonstration. After a few shows, I realised that the pack contained a selection of sizes of these things. We were always using the biggest one on stage, but I pocketed one of the smallest size and at the crucial point of the demonstration, I produced this and said, "Actually, I think this would have done, Blowers." It took the old boy a bit by surprise when I first did it, but it became an easy way to guarantee a cheap laugh.

Meanwhile, in the lift, our hero had assessed the choice of buttons. Several floors down there was RES for restaurant, and below that REC for reception. That latter was the one he selected – carefully, as he says, "because my life depended upon it". The lift set off, descending with encouraging speed. "I felt I was rounding Tattenham Corner in the Derby, well placed, with a gap in front and Lester Piggott on top. What could possibly go wrong? And then the bloody thing stopped!"

On the control panel, he could see that it had reached RES for restaurant. The doors took an agonising time to shudder and open. And there, in a mass in front of the open doors, were six men in dinner jackets and six ladies in evening dresses, all of them "irretrievably pissed". They took in the spectacle of Blowers, strategically clutching his doily and, after a moment of frozen astonishment, decided that they would all pelt him with crusty bread rolls that they found handily by the lift doors. "Fortunately," says Henry, "they were so far gone that their aim was a bit wayward and not too many rolls met their mark."

Eventually a man came to the rescue through the crowd. "You seem to be in a spot of bother," he said.

"How frightfully quick of you to spot it," said Blowers. "The man I'm really after is the night porter." He quickly realised that this was not necessarily an encouraging line.

"Hold the doors open," said the rescuer, "and I'll fetch him."

Now Henry had to risk his two-handed clutch on the doily to press the *DOORS OPEN* button. And still the bread rolls were coming from a seemingly inexhaustible supply. Spectator numbers also appeared to be increasing. "People were arriving by the coachload. They were selling tickets!" insists Blowers.

At last the night porter arrived to save him, though, as the buttons had been pressed, the lift had to go down to the ground floor and back to the restaurant en route to the safety of the tenth floor and the persecutors and their bread rolls took their chance to continue the merry assault.

At last he was restored to his room and, in the morning, he felt that he should go and apologise to the hotel manager for the night's chaos.

"Oh, never mind," said the manager. "It's not the first time something like that has happened and I'm sure it won't be the last. There is one thing, though, about the positioning of your doily. In my experience, most people, I find, are recognised principally by their faces."

On the subsequent tour of *Rogues on the Road*, we decided that this story went down so well that it became an ideal one to close the first act on.

At this 2015 Edinburgh Fringe, we were starting our run midway through the festival, which had probably helped with the advance publicity and we were surprised and very gratified on the first day to see a long queue waiting to get into our late-afternoon show. It was a wonderful start, though inevitably audiences of over two hundred could not be maintained throughout, which got Blowers rather grumpy. The fact is that, financially, it is very difficult to do better than break even at the Fringe. The Spiegeltent, because of its circular shape, was a slightly odd house to play and, while we were used to performing in front of audiences we couldn't see, with the lights in our eyes, the stained-glass windows meant we could see them clearly. It made for a rather different approach and interaction.

Our commentary clips now included Christopher Martin-Jenkins in New Zealand describing Daniel Vettori refusing to be drawn into fishing outside the off stump. "He stays on the bank and keeps his rod down – so to speak." Without the 'so to speak', he probably would have got away with it, but as it was, he corpsed. Nor was Jeremy Coney, his expert summariser, any help at all. In the background on the recording can be heard the voice of Aggers, the architect of the leg-over incident, saying, "Good luck."

We led into the subject of John Arlott with talk – inevitably – of drink being taken. Blowers had a good yarn about going to Pakistan armed with two bottles of whisky and having them confiscated at the customs desk at Karachi Airport. A couple of evenings later he met at a reception a man who introduced himself as Commander Jalani, head of customs at the airport. "Ah!" said Henry. "You owe me two bottles of Scotch", and told him the story.

The commander laughed. "Oh, those will have been drunk long ago." But he told Blowers to let him know when he was next coming and he would smooth his way.

He did not have too long to wait. On his next visit, Blowers prepared the way, was reassured that all would be well and armed himself this time with four bottles. When he arrived, he was met by the commander's assistant and escorted to the office and, while he enjoyed a glass with his friend, his immigration and customs were expedited. He was even given the use of the commander's car to get him to his hotel.

That evening, as he was contemplating a snifter from the first bottle in his hotel room, the phone rang. A lady announced herself as being in reception where a Commander Jalani was asking for him. "Oh, yes!" he said. "Splendid fellow! Send him up."

In the session that followed they made very quick work of demolishing that first bottle.

Next evening, at about the same time, the call from reception came again. "Commander Jalani is here to see you." This time they might have taken five minutes longer to see off bottle number two.

The third bottle went the same way next evening, but Blowers was wise enough by now to have hidden the fourth and regretted to the commander that it had already been disposed of. Not long after that he met at a party an English businessman who frequently flew in and out of Karachi. Henry told him the tale. "Oh, you've met Commander Jalani!" the businessman said. "He's done that to me several times."

The John Arlott sound extract I had selected was from the Centenary Test in Melbourne in 1977. He was painting a wonderful picture of Dennis Lillee bowling to Derek Underwood, with the silver gulls standing in line, "like vultures for Lillee". Underwood managed to get Lillee away for a boundary; "and it's not often that Underwood hits Lillee for four. And there was a brief exchange of what are usually called 'pleasantries'."

I would get into this clip by telling why Arlott had only ever done one full tour of Australia (in truth, he was not a happy tourist and he hated the heat). But the tale was that early on during the 1954/5 tour – I placed it in Perth, but I was not entirely sure that that was the city in question – he was having an abstemious dinner on his own in the hotel. So he only ordered two bottles of claret. The waiter brought one and poured him a glass, leaving the bottle on the table. He then started to beat a retreat.

Arlott beckoned him back. "Excuse me, my man," he said. "I ordered two bottles."

"That's all right, Mr Arlott," said the waiter. "The second bottle's in the freezer."

On our subsequent autumn tour, audience reaction to this line was interesting. In Wimborne, for instance, there was a pained groan from them, while there were places where we felt the need to explain in advance that claret should be served at room temperature. That was a reaction we used in the telling. I might say, "In Wimborne they groaned, but in Warrington they couldn't understand the problem."

I would lead into a clip of Brian Johnston with a tale of him flying out to Australia in the 1960s, when the plane had to make a few refuelling stops en route. One of these was in Bahrain, where he took the opportunity to walk up and down the transit lounge to get the feeling back into his legs. A man approached him as he was doing this, saying, "I'm sorry to interrupt you, but I know I've seen you before. No, no, don't tell me, I'll get it in a minute."

Brian, rather wearily, was reaching for a pen, ready to sign an autograph.

"I will get it in a minute," insisted the man. "It's on the tip of my tongue." Then, triumphantly, he exclaimed, "I know! Didn't you used to drive a bus in Watford?"

"Not," said Johnners, "in Watford."

For the sound clip I had him discussing the pigeons on the outfield on some ground, "looking for worms".

Bill Frindall chipped in, suggesting that pigeons were not carnivorous.

"Which means they wouldn't eat worms," said Johnners. "I bet if I offered a pigeon a nice juicy worm, he'd eat it. Would you do that for me, Boil?" he asked Trevor Bailey. "Would you find one of Blowers' thoughtful pigeons? Of course, we'd have to get a worm, too. I hadn't thought of that."

It was a splendid piece of *TMS* nonsense and, combined with Arlott's earlier reference to the Melbourne gulls, it led on to Blowers recounting how, earlier the same year in Cardiff, he had been walking back to his hotel when some startled gulls had taken flight and "taken up a formation that the Red Arrows would have been proud of, flown over me and proceeded to deposit every bit of liquid or solid waste that they had". His new linen coat had apparently gone to the dry-cleaners to be declared irretrievable. "Sheer, naked ingratitude!" declared the outraged world's leading commentator on avian activity on cricket grounds.

Shortly before coming to Edinburgh, Henry had been to lunch at Buckingham Palace. He had been telling the Queen how much he enjoyed Edinburgh during the festival. "Except," he said, "that the Royal Mile does get so uncomfortably crowded."

"I live on the Royal Mile," Her Majesty responded, with a twinkle in the eye.

This year the 'Talent v Industry' cricket match on the Meadows was able to take place, with Blowers in splendid form as the commentator, many strange things happening not usually seen on a cricket field, and the whole thing ending appropriately as a tie, with agreement all round that we must do it again next year.

Indeed, there was plenty of "See you next year" going on when we left after our two-week run in the Spiegeltent, which we had become quite fond of. Audiences had not, in the end, been too bad and we had got the basis of our new show ready for the autumn tour.

- 13 -

Roadwork for the Rogues

OUR PROPOSED SCHEDULE FOR the autumn of 2015 consisted of thirty-two shows in two months, stretching from Exeter to Aberdeen. A couple were eventually postponed to the following spring, but it promised to involve plenty of mileage. In fact, my car insurers, after asking for precise details of what I was doing, decided to put my occupation down as 'full-time comedian', which got a bigger laugh from my family than any story we told on stage.

Before we embarked on our travels round the country, we had planned a run-through with a performance at the Hen & Chickens at Highbury Corner again. The overcrowded bar on the night was encouraging, but it turned out that only one of the drinkers was expecting to come upstairs to the theatre. All the rest were there to go on to Arsenal's home European Cup game at the Emirates Stadium. So we just ran through a few things for ourselves and Emma Brünjes' benefit.

After an opening show in Maidenhead, we did the three 'W's – not so much Weekes, Worrell and Walcott as Wimborne, Wolverhampton and Warrington – on consecutive nights. It was as good an example of the variations in venues as possible. The first an enthusiastic volunteer-run theatre, with a guaranteed full house; the second a sort of jazz club atmosphere, with a bar at the back; and the third a council-run arts centre.

Our Wolverhampton stage was in the Slade Rooms, for which title the penny did not drop until I reached the green room behind the stage, which was adorned with large pictures of Noddy Holder and the boys in their younger days. Only then did I remember that Slade were a Wolverhampton group. Our night in Warrington was mainly memorable for it taking place in a monsoon. After unloading the car, I needed wringing out and so did most of the stage set.

Two nights later we were in Melton Mowbray at a theatre attached to the college, which somehow never makes for a good audience. Happily, being just down the road from the Agnews ensured us the presence of two more. If I had not seen via tweets in the morning that Emma and Jonathan were planning to come, I would have known when I recounted a story we had recently added to the repertoire.

It came at the end of a sequence which we had started for this tour, which began with Blowers telling the tale of being appointed 'social secretary' for a Derrick Robins cricket tour of South America, which involved several eye-opening scrapes, including the team captain,

Chris Cowdrey, losing his clothes in unfortunate and embarrassing circumstances during the course of a match in Rio.

I went on from that to the occasion of Cowdrey's first Test Match in Bombay in 1984, when he was brought on to bowl for the first time. His father, Colin, later to become Lord Cowdrey of Tonbridge, was apparently driving through Lewisham, listening – of course – to *Test Match Special.* The story went that he was so excited by this news that he turned the wrong way up a one-way street, where he was quickly stopped by a policeman.

As he was explaining that his son had just started to bowl his first over in Test cricket, Cowdrey Junior clean-bowled the great Kapil Dev. Culprit and guardian of the law cheered together and the policeman sent him on his way, though not without the cautionary words, "Good job you've got a famous son."

As that Test was being played in Bombay on the ground where I saw my first overseas Test Match – and, indeed, the ground on which I produced *TMS* for the last time in India – we went on to comment on the fact that over the quarter of a century between those two matches, I did not reckon the commentary box had been cleaned once. The layer of pigeon shit looked very familiar, as did the half of a dead rat.

Blowers ventured the thought that it had not been cleaned since Queen Victoria's day, to which I could respond that he would know.

On my last visit there, for the 2006 Test Match, I remember Aggers' opening words on the first morning.

"Good morning, everyone. Welcome to *Test Match Special*. There are cricket grounds round the world whose name gives a good idea of the nature of the place. You think of the Rose Bowl and you get an idea of Hampshire's bucolic charm. The Riverside suggests the River Wear slipping peacefully past, and, of course, Lord's gives a suggestion of nobility." He paused. "Into this category easily falls Bombay's Wankhede Stadium."

While that always went down well, on this occasion in Melton Mowbray, a familiar voice came out of the darkness of the auditorium. "My solicitors are listening!"

Within the next fortnight, two other *TMS* colleagues came to see the show: Vic Marks in Exeter and Johnny Saunders, who had now left the BBC to become a schoolmaster, in Newbury. Their reactions were rewardingly similar – both seeming surprised that they had enjoyed it so much.

The wonderful contrasts of a theatre tour continued with, on consecutive nights, the modern, functional Andover Lights; the grand old-fashioned Theatre Royal in Lincoln; the intimate Swindon Arts Centre and the forbidding Wycombe Town Hall. The latter was even worse than I had remembered it from our previous visit. I walked round the building to see if anyone could get a clue from the exterior that there was any sort of show on that night or, indeed, that it was still in use for anything. There was none, so the disappointingly small audience was only to be expected.

Although they had confirmed to the agents that they could hang our map backdrop, it was clear that they could not. Fortunately, it was a problem I had foreseen might occur one day and so I had acquired a system of supports, which, while not quite tall enough to show the whole thing, could nonetheless display the business area. Some of the problem of the venue's attitude might have been explained when I overheard the stewards being briefed by their boss. "Tonight we have a cricket talk." Oh dear.

Those map supports were again needed for a remarkable evening we had on the *Cutty Sark*. We were in the lower hold, with minimal headroom, our low platform arranged down the port side of the ship. By contrast, our dressing room was the very roomy upper hold and Blowers and I were able to stride the deck before the show, like seafarers of old. Then down below to a wonderfully cosy atmosphere with a full-house audience of ninety, through which we had rather to force our way to get on stage. It made for a very different, but thoroughly enjoyable evening for us – and, I hope, for the audience.

We were building up for another West End appearance, this time at the Duchess Theatre, just off Covent Garden. The two nights before that saw us in Devon and the Isle of Wight, the latter being in a university theatre on the outskirts of Newport on a dispiritingly wet Sunday evening. It was a perfect storm of the features that make for a poor audience. For most of the show, indeed, it was missing two. The couple we were staying with had gone into Newport some time after we had left the house for our venue and they had gone to the theatre they knew. They were not put off by the absence of their promised tickets left on the door and talked their way in. They then sat through a song-and-dance routine, which they presumed must be our warm-up act. However, when it reached an interval, they checked on whether we were following and discovered that they were in the wrong place. They arrived in our theatre just before we got to the question session at the end of the show.

For this tour we had changed our 'planted' last question. I would put it to Blowers that someone wanted to know how close a relation he was to the Bond villain, Ernst Stavro Blofeld. As he would say mischievously, "the one who is always seen stroking the white pussy".

"My mother," he would start, "always regarded Ernst Stavro as 'part of the castle not normally shown to visitors.'" He would tell how Ian Fleming had settled down one evening to write a book that became *Thunderball* and found himself searching for a name for an evil villain. "So he went to bed, scratching his head, which isn't the best way to get to sleep." The next day he went to his club in St James's Street, settled himself in an armchair and called for the membership list. There, among the 'B's, he found "a phalanx of three Blofelds" – Henry, his brother John, and their father. With that he "gave a yelp of joy, slammed the book shut, called for a glass of champagne and never looked back".

This story had been related to Blowers by Fleming himself at a lunch party in Jamaica when Blowers was on honeymoon – for the first time. Also at the lunch was Noël Coward, who subsequently invited the young newly married Blofelds to dinner at his small Jamaican retreat. Blowers enchantingly told how, after the meal, Coward went to the piano and played and sang 'Don't Put Your Daughter on the Stage, Mrs Worthington', 'The Stately Homes of England' and 'Mad Dogs and Englishmen'. And, as Blowers says, "It doesn't get much better than that."

To follow that, our last story of the show, we used 'Mad Dogs and Englishmen' as the music to see us off the stage. It seemed appropriate not only for that story, but to follow the accounts of touring misbehaviour.

Not all the stories were of bad behaviour, though. On his first cricket tour as a journalist, in India in 1963/4, Blowers found he was following an England team beset by injury and illness as it came to the second Test in Bombay. The day before the Test he attended a press conference, after which he was asked to stay behind by the captain, Mike Smith and manager, David Clark. Clark told him that they were struggling to find eleven fit men from the playing party to take the field next day. Only he and Henry of the rest had ever played first-class cricket and Blowers, being twenty years younger, was the better bet. He was asked to "Try to get to bed before midnight", just in case he was needed.

Blowers made one stipulation. He knew that Colin Cowdrey and Peter Parfitt were flying out as reinforcements, but he said, "If I make fifty or above in either innings, I'm damned if I'm standing down for Calcutta."

Clark was reserved in his response. "That, dear boy," he said, "is a fence we will jump when we get to it."

Having succeeded in his first task of making the bedtime deadline, Blowers reported to the dressing room at the

Brabourne Stadium in good time in the morning. However, Micky Stewart rose from his hospital bed just in time to deprive the tyro of his Test cap, though he only managed a brief time on the field before he had to be returned to the hospital. As Blowers says, "My patriotism did not extend to fielding as twelfth man." India lent the tourists a player to do that job, by the name of Kripal Singh.

There had been another, similarly disappointing, let-down for Henry a few days earlier. At one of the many parties and receptions which used to be such a part of cricket tours of the subcontinent, he had met a gorgeous Bollywood actress called Aisha. He had been moved to invite her to have dinner with him and she had promised to check her filming schedule and let him know the following night at the next reception they were both due to attend. A date was made and Blowers, very excitedly, booked a table at a top restaurant.

On the appointed evening, as he waited, he fortified himself with a couple of dry martinis, before he saw the object of his desire, looking stunning in a beautiful sari, being led towards him by the maître d'hôtel. To his surprise, bringing up the rear of the procession was a very much more mundanely sari-clad older woman – Blowers unkindly described her as "an old crone". He assumed this lady must be some sort of servant, there to look after Aisha's handbag or shawl.

To his surprise, Aisha asked the maître to pull up a third chair at the table for the 'crone'. Blowers made an attempt to kiss his proposed conquest on the cheek, but she swayed elegantly out of the way with more accomplishment than

Geoff Boycott avoiding a bouncer and said, "Henry, I don't think you've met my mother."

The situation was already looking a lot less promising than Blowers had hoped, before she revealed that her mother spoke no English, so that she had to translate everything into Hindi for the maternal benefit and the sparse, terse responses had to be translated into English, none of which made for flowing repartee.

"She was a greedy old bat, too," says Henry. "She had caviar to start. Then she opted for a double helping of caviar for the main course and yet another in place of a pudding." Now he was beginning to worry also about his tour expenses.

As his guests were leaving, he shook the mother's bony hand and she leaned forward and said, in perfectly good English, "We shall not be meeting again."

Subcontinental misunderstandings were a rich vein to tap. There was the occasion, during the 1996 World Cup in India, Pakistan and Sri Lanka, when I travelled up from covering a day/night game in Karachi, to do another in Lahore. Lahore's airport was yet to undergo its subsequent substantial facelift and the aircraft would park some way from the terminal building. A bus would then transport passengers to what passed for a baggage hall, where a system of antique conveyor belts would, in the fullness of time, be loaded with their luggage.

On this day, however, the luggage was painfully slow to arrive. We stood – or in my case, paced – around for a good half-hour, staring at the immobile conveyor belts.

As half an hour headed towards three-quarters, the only patient people were the porters, leaning on their trolleys, taking such delays as part of life's rich tapestry.

I was anything but patient, totally forgetting Kipling's warning about *A fool lies here, who tried to hustle the East*. And as I paced, I muttered, "Honestly, this lot couldn't organise a piss-up in a brewery."

A nearby porter overheard. "You want toilet?" he offered helpfully.

Blowers could add to this his account of travels during the previous World Cup in that part of the world, in 1987, when he had taken a number of journeys in company with Trevor Bailey. As they attempted to take a flight from Delhi to Nagpur during the tournament, Blowers was stung for excess baggage. He tried, after losing the lengthy bargaining process, to pay by credit card. They were having none of that and insisted on cash, which raised the temperature of the steam coming out of his ears and the force of his outburst of protestation.

Trevor was stern in his admonishment on the perils of losing one's temper in such circumstances. When they settled on the plane, he showed Henry his special newly issued platinum credit card which never failed, he explained, to be accepted everywhere.

Two days later they were checking out of their Nagpur hotel. Confidently, Trevor produced the magic new credit card. The hotel cashier vehemently refused to accept it. Trevor's previous cool evaporated and he exploded. Afterwards, he looked shamefacedly at Blowers. "I know," he said, "I didn't do very well."

That tale led into my own credit-card story. Leaving the Hotel Metro 35 in Chandigarh (no better than it sounds) in 1996, I offered the receptionist the choice of traveller's cheques or credit card. "Cash," he said.

"Is there a bank where I can change some traveller's cheques, then?"

He brightened. "Oh yes, just across the road."

"Well hang on, I'll just go and do that."

I was almost out of the door when he added, helpfully, "Bank is closed today."

As we had spent most of our time in Pakistan, I was low on Indian rupees, so we were back to the original choice of payment method. Eventually, after checking several times that I really did not have sufficient hard cash, he opted for the card. The slip was swiped through the machine and I was invited to sign it. The receptionist studied the signature on the slip and the one on the back of the card. Then, very deliberately, he took from his desk a ruler and measured the two signatures. "Is not the same," he said mournfully.

"Can't you see how small you have to write on the card strip?" I protested. It took some time and he was none too sure he was making the right decision, but at long last he accepted it.

An earlier visit to Chandigarh for a One Day International had revealed the press box being sited directly behind the sight screen. The entire ground was obscured from view. Naturally the leader of our press corps pointed out to local officials the problem with this arrangement. The man in charge was mystified. "I was told to put press box in line wicket to wicket," he insisted. "You can't get more in line than that!"

We decamped to the roof of the pavilion by way of a precarious ladder.

I once heard from Mike Brearley one of those disarming stories of Indian logic. He was Tony Greig's vice-captain for England's very successful tour of India in 1976/7. Taking over the captaincy of the side for one of the early upcountry games of the tour, he was in the field on the first morning when, after an hour's play, a drinks interval was called. Making the most of the occasion, rather than just the twelfth men coming on with a few water bottles, an army of be-turbaned waiters processed onto the ground with trays of various drinks. The players gathered round and it turned into something of a cocktail party.

After about five minutes, with no sign of the break coming to an end, Brearley felt that, leading England for the first time, he ought to take a bit of control of the situation. So he approached the umpires, suggesting that some dispatch was needed. He was told, "What is five minutes, compared with eternity?"

One does encounter a bit of eternity on a tour of India.

- 14 -

Last Orders

IN THE EARLY SUMMER of 2016, I had a phone call from Emma Brünjes' brother, Ralph, who had taken over as our day-to-day agent. They had decided that it was not a good idea for us to go to the Edinburgh Fringe that year, for what would have been our fourth season. The financial balance just did not add up.

Actually, it never had added up, but the exposure was sometimes worthwhile. For me, I think I just enjoyed the buzz of the place and the event and it probably helped to raise our profile in promoting the shows elsewhere. Now a little voice in my head was telling me that this might be the beginning of the end of our two-man show.

By that time we had already completed a spring tour, which had started at the beginning of March in a pub in Hertfordshire, which had presented a few problems. The map backdrop had to be gaffer-taped to the wall and the dressing room we were given was in real life the disabled loo. "What happens if a disabled person needs the loo?" I asked.

"They'll just have to hold it," was the landlord's unsympathetic reply.

The bar, I am proud to say, did exceptionally well that night, to the extent that, when the normal twenty-minute show interval had been going on for three-quarters of an hour, I sneaked a message out of the disabled loo to ask when we might get going again. Eventually we did.

Our next show involved an unfortunate piece of timing, being on Merseyside on a night when Liverpool were playing at home against Manchester United. The staff of the Epstein Theatre, so welcoming when we had performed there two-and-a-half years before, were for the most part rather hostile, making it fairly clear that they would rather have been watching the football. I mentioned to one of our audience at the post-show book signing that he must be an Everton fan to have chosen to come and see us. "Oh no," he said, "I was watching the match on my iPhone during the show."

Happily, the next night provided us with a warm Yorkshire welcome at the Otley Courthouse – a delightful little volunteer-run theatre, where our dressing room was the former judge's robing room and we were shown the old cells previously occupied by those awaiting trial.

We were revisiting several venues and discovering some which were new – to me, at least – like the Marine Theatre in Lyme Regis, outside which was a large banner advertising the Fossil Festival. It was a small relief to find that this was not an advertisement for our show.

We were clearly not quite what the Civic Arts Centre in Oswaldtwistle had been expecting. When I arrived, I was walked through a smallish low-ceilinged conference room where my guide said, "We were going to put you in here, but we sold too many tickets, so I'm afraid we've had to move you to the main theatre."

That was a good-sized auditorium, but, obviously still not understanding what we did, they had put an eighteen-inch-high platform in front of the stage for us to use. I made it clear that we would be much better served by being on the stage itself.

Those fifteen spring shows took us from Devon to North Yorkshire and a further ten evenings were booked for November, which included two full houses at contrasting venues at either end of the Humber Bridge. The Ropery at Barton-upon-Humber at the Lincolnshire end is a building a quarter of a mile long, with a theatre at one end and a cafe at the other. Its original purpose was, as the name implies, the making of ropes. Slightly bizarrely, we had to sneak round the outside of the building once the audience were settled, to make our entrance through the fire door at the back of the stage.

At the Yorkshire end of the bridge, we were in the village hall at North Ferriby only four days later. It was a slightly grander venue than you might expect from a village hall and they certainly did us well, though it was a little surprising to stumble into the local Women's Institute committee meeting in a room next to our dressing room.

Generally, what was to be our last autumn tour was very successful, but there was one all-too-memorable Saturday evening at what was presented to us as the Gloucester Comedy Festival. Our brief said only that the venue was King's School, Gloucester, and it was only when I got there that I discovered that King's School is one of those whose buildings are scattered through the city. Trying to identify which one might house our stage was impossible, and driving from one to another was not made any easier by the fact that Gloucester had a home rugby match that evening at Kingsholme. I even went into a pub where I expected to find posters for the festival, but no one had even heard of it.

Eventually, by chance, I ran into Blowers who, fortunately, had been armed with a contact number, so we were able to find the man who knew which school hall we were performing in. Our dressing room was a curtained-off corner of the stage itself, from where we were worried to hear so little pre-show conversation from the audience as they came in. When we went on stage, we discovered why. They numbered eighteen. I was able to count them while Blowers was telling his first story.

Worse than that, two of them were local journalists who disappeared at the interval. And all this after being told by the organiser that we were there as big names to launch their festival!

Early in 2017, Blowers rang to say that he was thinking of making this his last year on *Test Match Special*. He asked me what I thought, but it was obvious that his mind was made up. I recalled John Arlott – at a younger age than Henry – saying, "I'm going while they're asking, 'Why?' rather than waiting till they ask, 'Why not?'" *TMS* would certainly be losing a character and, for all the buses, pigeons, butterflies and "frightfully pretty" girls, someone who could be relied on to give the score more regularly than most.

He would be announcing his retirement in June, so for a few months I had a secret to keep, but soon after I heard that plan from him came the news that, after his retirement from the commentary box, he would be embarking on an autumn tour of a solo show. The Blofeld and Baxter double act was at its end.

It meant that little publicity effort was spent on our last three shows in the early summer. But Blowers had chosen to hang up his microphone in a significant year for *Test Match Special*. The end of May saw the programme's sixtieth anniversary. It was something of a shock for me, as I had retired from producing it on its fiftieth anniversary. Where had the last ten years gone? (Well, half of them had been spent touring theatres with H. Blofeld.)

I felt a little bow from us to the start of radio cricket commentary was appropriate, with a slightly lighter hand than we had used in our first show at Liscombe Park five years before and, in mentioning the early commentators, I was able to include a commentary extract from 1936. The BBC had decided that first-class cricket might be too dull for radio listeners. (Though the great pioneer of commentary Howard Marshall had commentated splendidly on England's win at Lord's over Australia two years before, when Hedley Verity had taken fourteen wickets in a day.) So they sent someone to cover a village match at Tilford in Surrey.

That commentator was one Tommy Woodroffe and he included, in pre-*TMS* style, a description of the tea they had had. "I had some myself, as a matter of fact." He then had Eddie the fast bowler coming in with the sound of a tractor and ducks quacking in the background. But he complained of not finding it easy to give the score, because it was raining and the small boy who operated the scoreboard didn't like the rain.

That clip enjoyed by the audience, we would then reveal more about the career of Woodroffe. The following year he was selected to commentate on the royal review of the fleet at Spithead. The choice was made because he had previously been an officer in the Royal Navy. Probably unfortunately for him, the vessel chosen to be his commentary position was his old ship, HMS *Nelson*, and there were still former brother officers aboard. They entertained him rather too royally in the wardroom before his broadcast, with the result that his subsequent efforts went down in history as, "The fleet's lit up!"

That was his most-remembered phrase, as he lurched through his commentary, describing it as, "Like fairyland." At one stage he had to tell some people behind him to, "Shut up." I assume they might have been trying to drag him off the air, but, as I would tell audiences, somehow he was allowed to go on for about seven minutes, when it was quite clear that he was comprehensively the worse for drink. We only gave them a very shortened version of the original and it would lead us into some of our tales of the perils of mixing alcohol and broadcasting.

Our last show together was at the Oxford Festival of the Arts at the beginning of July, soon after the announcement of Blowers' retirement had been made public. We were in a large marquee by the river, where he got a splendid reception on the back of the wave of public regret that such a voice of summer would be silenced. I was able to tease him about the obituaries I seemed to have been reading about him.

Tributes were pouring in. The Prime Minister Theresa May, no less, invited to contribute to a programme celebrating *TMS*'s sixtieth birthday, added a personal tribute to "Blowers, my dear old thing".

His book, *Over and Out,* was published and started flying off the shelves, and then, on 9th September, appropriately at Lord's, the great man finished his final commentary spell. Characteristically, he got tangled up with his microphone headset as he tried to make an elegant departure. Then he was summoned to join Jonathan Agnew and Vic Marks at the pavilion end of the ground, where they were dealing with post-match presentations and interviews. His progression in front of the Mound and Tavern Stands was remarkable, as if he and not England had just beaten the West Indies in the Test Match. He was cheered to the echo and responded with regal waves to the crowd. He was even invited to take champagne with the team in the England dressing room.

It echoed the departure of John Arlott a little, though I did reflect sadly that neither Brian Johnston nor Christopher Martin-Jenkins had been able to schedule their own farewells.

Happily for Blowers, as he hurries towards the end of his eighth decade, there seems to be plenty left in the tank and I look back on my time with him by echoing the title of Johnners' first autobiography, *It's Been a Lot of Fun.* And acknowledging that we have been very lucky!